Freedom from Darkness

Praise for *Freedom from Darkness*

"Teresa Yanaros brings a hard-earned knowledge of the occult to help others make the journey to freedom, as she has. Pastoral care before and after deliverance or exorcism is the big piece that is so far missing. Teresa speaks in terms that people understand to help them break free of internal bondage so that they are more likely to reach out for help from their dioceses. Through work like hers, more people will wake up to the lies of the occult and seek the freedom and peace that come in a relationship with Jesus Christ."

— **Adam Blai, Author, *The Exorcism Files***

"Here is a thorough introduction to the world of occult practices and New Age movements. Teresa takes us through the many stages of occult bondage and deliverance in this book as she narrates her personal struggle for healing and deliverance from the occult realm. Her book is an excellent resource for people working in the deliverance ministry as well as for those who have been victims of occult practices. Let us not be deceived by the foolish lies of the evil one but always cling to our God, who is the Father of truth, hope, and love."

— **Fr. Joseph Royan, C.Ss.R., S.T.L.,**
Director and editor, Redemptorist Publications India

"If you've gone down the wrong spiritual path and need help finding freedom in Christ, read this book!"

— **Fr. Mark Goring, C.C., Speaker and writer**

"An insightful exploration of the subtle yet significant battles in our spiritual lives, Teresa Yanaros's compelling testimony of deliverance from occult influences offers practical guidance for deepening our prayer lives and embracing God's will in the midst of spiritual warfare. Her work underscores the vital importance of surrendering our thoughts and purposes to Jesus and steadfastly submitting to the sacraments as the primary pathway to true freedom."

— **Dan Burke, Author, *The Devil in the Castle***

Teresa Yanaros

Freedom from Darkness

A Roadmap to Deliverance from Spiritual Bondage and the Occult

SOPHIA INSTITUTE PRESS
Manchester, New Hampshire

Cover design by Emma Helstrom.

On the cover: Watercolor clipart (2307147271), image derived from Hearts and Peaches / shutterstock.com; black silhouette of Jesus (1705837438), image derived from KOV777 / shutterstock.com; abstract flare light (2482411775), image derived from oscargutzo / shutterstock.com.

Image on page 106 by artist 3Satva.

Sophia Institute Press
Box 5284, Manchester, NH 03108
1-800-888-9344
www.SophiaInstitute.com

Sophia Institute Press is a registered trademark of Sophia Institute.

paperback ISBN 979-8-88911-492-5

ebook ISBN 979-8-88911-493-2

Library of Congress Control Number: 2024951333

First printing

This book is dedicated to the Blessed Virgin Mary.

You were a sign to me in my darkness to keep going,
to keep running into the arms of your beloved Son, Jesus.
May the Seven Sorrows of your Immaculate Heart
be a beacon of light for all afflicted persons and
a blessed reminder to always cling to the perfect
and efficacious Blood of Christ.
Pray for us sinners, now and
at the hour of our death. Amen.

Contents

Part 2: Path to Freedom

Foreword

It is often said that the devil's greatest weapon is disbelief in him. As long as his works stay under the radar and he is dismissed as a myth or fairy tale, he can carry out his diabolical project in human souls undercover and undetected. When, however, a light is shone on his vicious scheming and insidious attacks, he loses the power that darkness affords him. Recent research suggests that his efforts to conceal himself have been quite successful, and even among Christians, some 40 percent strongly agreed that Satan "is not a living being but is a symbol of evil."[1]

If you doubt the existence of Satan, I dare you to read this book.

Teresa Yanaros has given the world a priceless gift by sharing the intimate and compelling story of her personal experience of occult bondage and demonic oppression, as well as her even more important experience of the salvation offered by Jesus Christ.

This is also a vital wake-up call for those who dally in the occult, thinking that such activities are harmless pastimes rather than dangerous dealings with the demonic. As C. S. Lewis wrote, "The more a

1 "Most American Christians Do Not Believe That Satan or the Holy Spirit Exist," April 13, 2009, *Barna*, https://www.barna.com/research/most-american-christians-do-not-believe-that-satan-or-the-holy-spirit-exist/.

man was in the Devil's power, the less he would be aware of it, on the principle that a man is still fairly sober as long as he knows he's drunk."[2]

As dark as this topic is — and there is no exaggerating the truth to this — this book is ultimately a work of hope. Teresa's moving testimony gives hope to those tempted to despair and provides a valuable roadmap that highlights the path out of darkness and into light. As terrifying and sinister as the devil is, he is still a creature and no match for the supreme power of God.

This path begins with awareness of the truth of one's personal situation and the recognition of an enemy who works tirelessly to separate human beings from God. It continues to deliverance and metanoia, a "turning" away from evil and toward God. This involves purification from sin and the acceptance of God's mercy and grace. It also entails overcoming obstacles and persevering on the road of righteousness despite Satan's ongoing attempts to make us return to him.

On this journey, you could have no better travel companion than Teresa Yanaros, a true woman of God who knows the road, having fallen into plenty of potholes herself. As such, her words are not preaching from a soapbox, but gentle, firm counsel from a sister who wishes to share her own experiences of the spiritual warfare meant to lead all of us into the powerful, protective embrace of a loving God.

— Thomas D. Williams

[2] C. S. Lewis, *The Screwtape Letters* (New York: Harper One, 2001), 18.

Acknowledgments

The Holy Trinity. Thank You, Heavenly Father, for Your perfect plan of redemption. Thank You for giving me life so that I may turn around and glorify Your holy name. Jesus, thank You for deliverance! Thank You for Your precious blood that covers and sanctifies us. Holy Spirit, thank You for guiding us, guarding us, and inspiring us to keep our eyes locked on the Truth that is Christ. For the kingdom, the power, and the glory are Yours, now and forever. Amen!

Claudia Volkman. I would like to express a tremendous amount of gratitude to my editor, Claudia Volkman. Claudia, you have a ridiculously impressive gift for technical editing and, thanks to your expertise and precision, we were able to bring this dense package of material to the world. This project would not have been the same without you. You amaze me, and I am ever so grateful that the Lord brought you into my life, and into the fold to help me bring this work to fruition. Your ability to whip this level of a project into shape blew me away, time after time. You are seriously the best and every part of working with you is a delight.

Thomas D. Williams. I can't express in words how much your support is a beacon of light to me. As soon as I began to witness flickers of hope that my work was moving toward book publication, your words of encouragement continually brought me back to the path of resilience and clarity. As soon as you became aware of this project, you have championed it, protected it, prayed for it, and remained a voice of firm confidence. When God revealed to me that you were the perfect fit to write the foreword, everything came together. The book was planted into its proper place, to join the fight, to light the way, not just for those coming out of the occult, but for Christians experiencing persecution, no matter the flavor. I am emphatically stoked about our collaborations.

Noelle and Jamie. The Lord gave me two of the most important cherished gifts I've ever received when He introduced the two of you into my life. From day one, we've been through a wild journey of transformation. I cannot effectively express how proud I am of y'all for being brave enough to walk the walk and step forward to share the hearts of your stories to the world. Your voices are truly inspirational, offering beautiful songs of love to our Lord. You teach others how to stand in the light of Christ by dancing in joyful surrender and living out the faith. Thank you for the countless hours of counsel you have both provided me as I worked through extremely complex concepts and creating new nomenclature from scratch in the attempt to capture our experiences in a way that can best impact the world. Y'all's wisdom, growth, introspection, feedback, love, compassion, brilliance, and charity have changed my life and made this project possible. I love you both, from the bottom of my heart. Vaca Sisters for life. "Jesus, I trust in you!"

Fr. Joseph Royan, C.Ss.R. Thank you for expertly understanding the vision and praying ceaselessly over this operation. Your wisdom in Christ, spiritual direction, and friendship have blessed me. You've been a truly wonderful guiding shepherd and protective cover over this ministry. God bless you, Father.

Family and Friends. From the bottom of my heart, thank you to each of the academy students, especially Spencer, Krista, Leslie, Chelsea, and Teal. This journey was made possible because of the truly remarkable incubator we've cultivated over these past few years. Your friendship, support, and creativity have allowed this vision to bloom. Thank you to Dan Burke representing strong Catholic community and providing an arsenal of guidance, advice, and strategies along the way. I offer my deepest appreciation to Adam Blai for his attention to detail and intentional review of my work. Thank you for seeing the value in this ministry and offering critical mentorship when I needed it most. Thank you to Sarah Lemieux for being a beacon of light in the early stages of the academy and onward, for offering support and resources and opening up pathways of healing for the students. A special thank-you to my family, John, Eileen, Shelley, Valerie, Mark, Colin, Kelly, and Bev, for loving me truly and fully, and always cheering me on. A deeply heartfelt thanks to Emma, Jenna, Walt, Zach, and Jesse for holding me during the darkest moments of bondage and pointing the way to the Lord at all times.

My Aunt Emma. Emma, you were there picking up the broken pieces in my darkest hours of deliverance. You opened the door and took me in during my hardest and most confusing points of gaining freedom from the occult. Your Christian influence helped tether me to the rock of Christ and untangle the occult worldviews from my mind. Thank you for the countless hours you spent sitting on the couch with me, poring over Scripture and bringing light to the darkness. You are an incredible woman. I adore you.

My Father, John. Thank you for believing in me and always being there to remind me how important it is that we surrender to the Lord and heed the call to help others. Thank you for teaching me to look deeper. Thank you for cheering me on when I felt discouraged. You have shown me the Father's love. I love you with my heart and soul.

My Mother, Eileen. I wouldn't be where I am without your prayers and direction. You are truly the best mother in the world and have always told me since I was a little girl, "Teresa, you are going to publish a book one day." And here we are. Thank you for the countless hours of deep conversation we've shared about theology, Catholic living, and deliverance. Thank you for loving me and being my primary cheerleader, every single step of the way. I love you with all of me!

Prologue

Deliverance from Evil

What if this is all demonic?

The words hit me like a shock to my system. As soon as the realization occurred, the demons, now caught, turned on me.

The gig was up.

Immediately, it was as if Hell was standing in my room. Demons were laughing at me, jeering at me, intimidating me. I couldn't get their voices out of my head. It was as though someone had flipped a switch and everyone was suddenly screaming at the top of their lungs.

The demons had concealed themselves from me by many masks to attempt to pull me into various conspiracist and ufological narratives. They presented as blue-gray aliens, large and small bird beings, Nordic-looking humans, and a litany of other shapes and sizes. But now, they were grotesque monsters, closing in on me from all sides.

For the first time in a long time, I ran and found a Bible. I curled up in the fetal position on my bed and prayed that God would show me something that would offer me a lifeline. I flipped the Bible open and began to read.

> The coming of the lawless one by the activity of Satan will be with all power and with pretended signs and wonders, and with all wicked deception for those who are to perish, because they refused to love the truth and so be saved. (2 Thess. 2:9–10)

The words impacted me to a degree I didn't anticipate. A gut-wrenching sob came from somewhere deep inside me. Suddenly, it was as though I were in outer space, standing at the very edge of reality. I became potently aware of my sin. I could feel in my body the reality of the choices I had made — every decision, every step away from God. It wasn't anything He did to walk away from me, but I had walked away from Him. Now I was drowning in my sin. Its stain was all over me — in my mind, in my body, in my heart, in my spirit. I felt cold. I was cast out into the eternal darkness because of my own wretchedness.

The depth of my sin overwhelmed me and threatened to drag me under. Satan sneered. Outer space became even colder and more desolate.

"*God, save me!*" I cried, from the deepest recesses of my soul.

Within a millisecond, I felt the Lord swoop in and cover every single crevasse of my room. Satan was gone, the demons were gone … everything was still.

God had answered my prayer.

Introduction

Why I Wrote This Book

This book is for the spiritual lepers:

- Those who have gone into occult bondage
- Those who have faced demonic oppression, vexation, or possession
- Those the Lord tore from the grasp of the enemy, carried by His own hand out of the pit of Hell, and established in His eternal Kingdom
- Those who have been delivered from the dominion of darkness and transferred through the precious Blood of Jesus into the Kingdom of God

You are seen.

This book is for you.

When someone leaves the occult and enters their local church, sadly they are often met with confusion, aversion, and a complete and utter lack of awareness of the reality of spiritual bondage. This leaves them in a horrible state. Where can they go to get help? How do they contextualize what they are going through? Who will believe them and walk alongside them and help them anchor their lives in Christ? Who will be prepared to offer guidance as they begin a very complicated journey out of occult bondage? They are often viewed in churches as what I call *spiritual lepers*. The recoil factor is real. This is a tragedy.

Although churches around the world are largely unprepared to handle these situations, the need to help people out of occult bondage will only increase. Christians must be equipped to respond to this need.

Occult Culture

The occult has been so normalized in our society that it's easier than ever before to be deceived, hook, line, and sinker, and drawn into occult traps. And it's happening to millions of people around the world.

Almost 20 percent of Americans, and a third of adults under the age of thirty, are unaffiliated with any religion, but identify as being spiritual in some way.

The growing desire to follow spiritual practices apart from the pursuit of Christ has created an environment deeply steeped in occult frameworks. The cultural push away from Christ's authority draws people of all generations to build whatever spiritual practices they want, constructing a worldview marked by relativism, universalism, and post-Christian beliefs. The foundation of these spiritual frameworks is constantly fluctuating, as they are built upon the ever-changing tenets of human hearts in this fallen world. The foundation of these practices is not the rock of Christ. The foundation of these practices leads to eternal death.

With access to occult items and manuals in major bookstores like Barnes and Noble, along with the billions of videos on social media platforms that teach witchcraft, exposure to the occult has saturated our culture. For example, TikTok, a platform marketed mainly toward Generation Z, hosts a plethora of videos presenting occult teachings to billions of viewers around the world.

> TikTok's #witch hashtag has received nearly 20 billion views, #witchtiktok has nearly two billion views, and #babywitch, a

> hashtag for those new to the craft, has more than 600 million views.[3]

And yet, Jesus is delivering lost souls out of the occult in droves! We must be prepared to meet the needs of these new and reformed believers, carry them into the Faith, spiritually form them, and help them anchor themselves in Christ.

The "Falling Away" Risk Factor

Unfortunately, some people who leave the occult to follow Christ fall away. I wrote this book to equip and bring clarity and context to those newly delivered from occult bondage, so the risk factor of falling away might be reduced to ash.

My vision is to champion and exhort ex-occultists to stay the course with Christ, walk the righteous path, endure to the end, and so be saved.

> You will be hated by all because of my name, but whoever endures to the end will be saved. (Matt. 10:22)

Getting free of the occult is not a one-and-done situation. It's a process. It takes dedication, motivation, and sincerity of heart. Additionally, post-deliverance requires a continuation of that dedication. Our sanctification process is lifelong and only ends when we are face-to-face with Our Lord Jesus Christ.

This is news to those who have encountered misinformation about deliverance and would seek to treat it as another occult healing methodology. They think they can grab a quick fix, get free of the demonic, and return to their old patterns and ways of life. Deliverance doesn't work like this.

[3] Mark Jones, "WitchTok: The Witchcraft Videos with Billions of Views," October 31, 2022, *BBC News*, https://www.bbc.com/news/newsbeat-63403467.

The occult is a set of practices and beliefs that put individuals in control and at the center. Surrendering that worldview and submitting to Christ as King takes these individuals out of the control seat. Christianity is not a list of practices and beliefs we follow to have control over our lives. It is surrender to the truth of the person Jesus Christ. Our profession of faith should be shouted from the rooftops as long as we have air in our lungs. Without the continued surrender of our heart to Jesus and openness to the indwelling of the Holy Spirit, we cannot embark upon the delightful journey of living out our faith. Empty procedures do not yield perseverance.

Assuming Radical Responsibility

Persevering in faith while leaving behind occult bondage presents unique challenges. The risk of falling away is extremely high due to spiritual affliction and the deeply ingrained impact of occult worldviews on the psyche. This is why a person who wishes to be freed must accept radical responsibility for the process.

I hesitate to even use the word *victim* when referring to those afflicted by the occult. I often ask people to remove this word from their vocabulary. Why? Because it can soften a person's acceptance of culpability. While there are some cases where a spiritual affliction is not caused by an action of the afflicted's own doing, the majority of cases I have seen are a direct consequence of occult involvement.

When a person becomes aware of their sin and starts to understand the nuances of why idolatry and pride grieve the Lord, it opens up the wounds in a way that allows the Lord to come in and heal them. Exchanging idolatry for Christ and pride for humility are the steps needed to cross the starting line of freedom — for good.

Who Am I and Why Do I Care?

I used to be an internationally recognized and touring New Age author, tarot card reader, and investigative journalist in the paranormal, New Age, and ufology fields.

I was heavily involved in witchcraft, tarot, divination, channeling, ufology, scrying, spellcrafting, crystal healing, reiki, ritual spellcasting, the law of attraction, manifestation, star families, starseeds, kundalini meditation, altered states of consciousness, astral travel, remote viewing, Ouija boards, seances, UFO ceremonies, and many other New Age and occult practices and beliefs. I was in contact with what I believed to be positive spiritual entities and extraterrestrials. The stuff worked! Little did I know these entities were demonic and under the power of Satan. I ignored red flags such as missing time, possessed states, demonic appearances, and vexation (not being able to contextualize what was happening).

Everything seemed to be going my way. I had TV show hosting offers and entertainment industry opportunities popping up everywhere.

Then it all came crashing down.

God started to reveal the evil in what I was doing and in the industry. I became aware of my sin. I looked the devil in the eye. I realized that I was fraternizing with demons. Once the gig was up, the demons revealed themselves as such and started attacking me with an intense fervor.

The Lord opened my eyes to Scripture. His truth poured into my life like a fire hose of life-giving water. Everything I read in the Bible was happening before my eyes. The false prophets. The idolatry. The evil. God vanquished the demonic strongholds in my mind and started to build me up with His truth. In the midst of spiritual warfare, demonic nightmares, and demonic vexation (demons leaving bruises on my body and attacking me), the Lord started to show me what to do. He revealed the idols all around me. I could feel them. I began destroying thousands of dollars' worth of books, tools, and objects. I burned my tarot business to the ground.

I started to come out against occult practices publicly, and powerful New Age leaders launched smear campaigns against me. (There's so much money involved in this field!) I was threatened and stalked. Professionals helped me to realize I was in the process of leaving a dangerous cult. I didn't know what a "cult" was until I left one and came against their lies and manipulation. Once I started researching what cults were and comparing this to what was happening to me, it began to make more sense and my eyes were opened. I realized this cult was actually satanism under the guise of New Age spirituality infused with ufology belief systems. I ended up having to move across the country for my own safety and that of my family.

I left the Internet and cut off almost all social contact for a year. Instead I spent time with the Lord and immersed myself deeply in the Bible. Surrounded by a small group of strong Christians who were gifted in healing and deliverance, I leaned into spiritual formation, Bible study, passage memorization, and theology. I read tons of books on deliverance, strongholds, and getting free of enemy influence. Spiritual warfare was happening all around me at this time, and God was in the long and arduous process of freeing me through the renewal of my mind.

I started asking Jesus to deliver me. One morning as I stood on a hill and prayed, I felt His presence, and I fell on my face. The whole world around me sang to Him in worship. Chains broke, and thousands of pounds of sin lifted! I felt Jesus take out my heart of stone and replace it with a new heart of flesh!

I returned to my hometown and enrolled in seminary to study theology and learn more about God. As I started sharing my Christian perspectives online, I was shocked to discover that New Age beliefs had permeated many Christian churches, too. Getting grounded in

Christ through all of this and learning how to spiritually discern what was orthodox and true was quite a process.

I anchored myself in a local Christian community and began working through even more layers of deliverance. I deepened my spiritual formation and returned to my roots of sacramental worship. As I leaned into the community aspects of Christian life, I attended training conferences, interviewed experts in Christian ministry, and started developing an arsenal of extensive resources to help others who were going through what I had gone through.

My Twofold Mission

The Lord called me into ministry to help those whom Jesus was freeing from the occult bonds of the New Age, and He gave me a twofold mission:

1. **To help Christians who have left the occult.** I help them rid themselves of occult/New Age influences, leading them from being mentally confused, emotionally dim, and spiritually oppressed to being theologically grounded and actively engaged in their relationship with God so they can confidently share the light of Christ with the world. I run an academy based on an effective liberation system I built. The latter half of this book will describe some of the methods and tools I offer to help people free themselves of occult influence.
2. **To increase awareness in Christian leaders about the New Age/occult side of spiritual warfare.** These things are not taught in seminary, but the normalization of occult practices in society is all around us. I have developed useful strategies and frameworks to provide Christians with the tools necessary to understand and teach these topics. I yearn to train and grow a network of advocates worldwide to respond to the growing need for spiritual direction for ex-occultists.

Combatting the Blend

The blending of the occult with Christianity is rampant, and the need for good education is paramount in combating misinformation. In truth, you cannot blend the occult with Christianity. There is no gray area. There is no middle ground. It's Jesus or else it isn't. Such syncretism is becoming increasingly commonplace in our churches, leading to serious spiritual issues.

Christians (both clergy and laity) can be prepared to minister to people around them who are confused about the occult and can provide an account with solid biblical backing to stand firm against the occult infiltration of the churches. I am passionate about serving as a bridge to help Christians fulfill that opportunity.

Using Testimony to Glorify God

Sharing one's testimony is a compelling way to evangelize souls. My own testimony goes into the deep, dark recesses of occult bondage and full possession. I stared Satan directly in the eyes, and then God called me out of bondage and delivered me out of Satan's evil clutches. Thus began a long and arduous process of deliverance. After going through my own deliverance and helping others get freed, I now teach about the power of testimony to spiritually multiply the Kingdom of God.

The academy's bread and butter teaches people how to go into the heart of a distorted worldview, contextualize it, and dismantle it. This process effectively identifies and then uproots old spiritual distortions. The structure helps them lead these purposes captive to Christ and identify theological truths that directly correspond to their own story, and it enables them to contextualize how God has moved and is moving in their life. It gives them clarity about their own life, and the confidence to turn and share that testimony with others in order to build up the

Kingdom. Once these kernels of wisdom are unlocked, they can share their journey with others in a way that makes the greatest impact.

This book will provide an understanding of the overarching deliverance roadmap that outlines an afflicted person's journey through the process of getting into and out of occult bondage and describes the nuances therein. Ultimately, it is a roadmap that shows the journey of enslavement to and freedom from the darkness of the occult. In each chapter, I will utilize my testimony as a case study to demonstrate how the deliverance process works.

1

The Deliverance Roadmap Overview

Deliverance is a process.

You might think that when a person has been in occult bondage for decades, they can hear the gospel, believe it, and — *BOOM* — they are instantly delivered and freed from the darkness of the occult.

I'm here to tell you that this is rarely the case. Yes, God is sovereign, and He can do anything. But getting free of occult bondage is an arduous process that often takes years of dedication and sanctification.

Through rigorous observation, I've found that deliverance can be boiled down to a framework of ten steps. The first five steps describe how a person gets into occult bondage. The next five steps explain how Jesus gets them out.

This book walks you through each of the ten steps of the deliverance process, which is designed to help:

- Readers fully grasp the intricacies of this process
- The afflicted who are going through deliverance
- Clergy and laypeople who are called to come alongside the afflicted as they walk with Christ through this intense journey

You Are Here

People coming out of occult bondage need a roadmap so they can determine where they are in the process of being freed from the darkness of the occult. I've created a diagram to help them figure out where they need to get anchored so they can zero in on the tools available to them at the right stage in the journey. Disorientation is a huge factor for people as they are coming out of the occult and various cults associated with it. *Confusion* is the single most common word people use to describe where they're at as they attempt to shake off what I call "New Age gunk" and ground themselves in Christ.

Having such a roadmap has been incredibly useful for people to understand where they've been and have hope for the future. Giving them a glimpse of what comes next helps them focus on the present. It inspires and motivates them to take the process of occult deliverance seriously so they can successfully get rid of occult worldviews and establish themselves as followers of Christ.

Here are brief descriptions of each section we will cover in depth across the span of this book.

Part 1: Into Occult Bondage

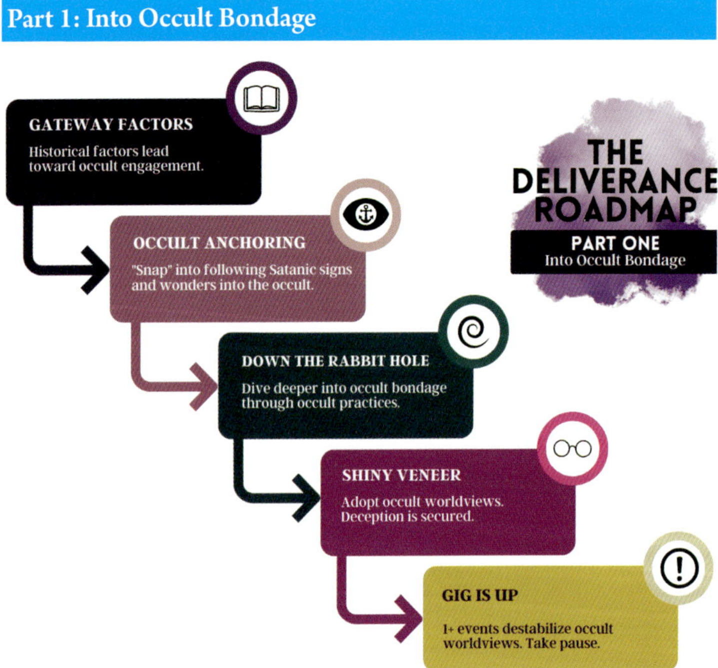

Gateway Factors

There are always historical factors that lead a person to get involved with the occult in any way.

These factors include family history, upbringing, traumatic events, and societal influences.

When a person assesses their past, they can usually identify worldly, traumatic, and occult factors that led to their interest in the occult.

Occult Anchoring

Occult anchoring is the five-step process by which Satan deceives humans, lie by lie, into occult bondage.

The five-step process: Lie > Curiosity > Doorway > Display > Anchor.

Each occult anchor is a lie accepted that installs a brick (distortion) in one's mind.

After the person accepts many bricks, these become strongholds of lies in the mind that eventually result in an occult worldview.

Occult Snapping

Occult snapping is a part of the occult anchoring process and occurs when a satanic sign or wonder "snaps" a person into believing that the occult is a viable and desirable path to traverse. I dedicated a full chapter to this because it is a core factor in occult deception.

At this point, the person is hooked and invested in following the path toward occult bondage.

Occult snapping is powerful because satanic signs and wonders destabilize a person's previously held worldview and leave them eager to understand the significance of the occult snapping event.

Due to the normalization of occult practices, practitioners often follow what they observe on the Internet and social media, or in popular media and books about how to get more involved in the occult.

Down the Rabbit Hole

After the person is snapped into the occult, they are now on a mission to seek what the occult offers: power, knowledge, healing, or a combination of these.

The person is continually drawn down the rabbit hole by a cycle of occult anchoring.

During this time, the person opens occult doors, makes demonic pacts, builds up strongholds of the mind, and then invites demons to attach to those strongholds through demonic invocation and evocation.

As the person goes deeper down the rabbit hole, the other parts of their life become increasingly less significant to them and their addiction to the occult sets in.

Shiny Veneer

"Even Satan disguises himself as an angel of light" (2 Cor. 11:14).

At this point, the person has bought into the shiny veneer the occult uses to hide the true nature of spiritual darkness. Believing the occult is good, they now hold occult worldviews.

A person's worldview is the lens through which they perceive reality. Built upon a worldview are a person's values, beliefs, thoughts, and attitudes, which fuel their emotions, actions, practices, and behaviors that lead to their habits and addictions.

An **occult worldview** is based on distortions about who the person is, who God is, and what a person's purpose is in the world. The core of this worldview is the attempt to seek the salvation of the person's soul through one's own actions and the achievement of self-serving goals.

The primary spirits that undergird the occult worldview are the spirits of delusion and antichrist.

"Gig Is Up" Moment

The person is now functioning inside an occult worldview.

Suddenly, an event occurs that destabilizes the occult worldview.

The "gig is up" moment occurs when a person begins to question the integrity of their worldview.

Sometimes the "gig is up" moment comes through the words of a friend, a well-placed phrase in a film or song, or perhaps a Bible verse spoken to them while their heart is in a softened state.

The "gig is up" moment rocks the person. It makes them stop and wonder if they are on the right path.

Part 2: Path to Freedom

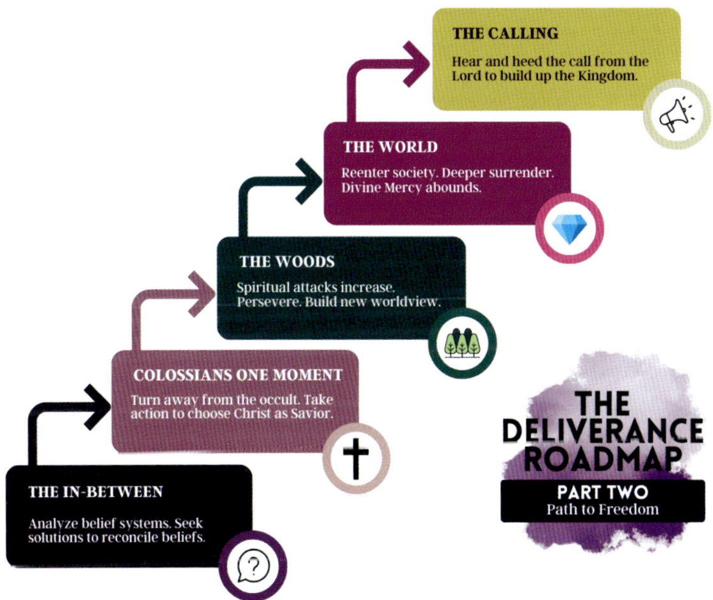

The "In-Between"

The "In-Between" is the lag time that often occurs after a "gig is up" moment and before the occultist actually turns to Christ for salvation.

Based on a person's upbringing, foundations, environmental factors, social group, and habits, they might try to find the solution elsewhere first.

Common places people turn to are worldly philosophies, sinful vices, and conspiracy media.

Some people only have one "gig is up" moment and then choose Christ. Others have multiple moments inside the In-Between before eventually coming to Christ.

Colossians One Moment

"He delivered us from the power of darkness and transferred us to the kingdom of his beloved Son, in whom we have redemption, the forgiveness of sins" (Col. 1:13).

The Colossians One Moment is when the person fully surrenders one's life to Christ.

This is often described as an enormous breakthrough or epiphany, when a person realizes the depth of the occult lie, and the truth that Jesus is the only way to eternal life hits their heart and breaks the chains of lies over their life.

The Woods

Enter

Spiritual warfare and demonic attacks typically increase when the afflicted enters what I call "the Woods." Satan loathes when an occultist comes to Christ, so he casts doubt and fear, trying to lure a person into isolation, suicide, and depression. Sometimes the attacks are so severe that Satan will try to kill the person.

The person must stay the course, stay strong, grounded in their faith, and persevere during this time of trauma and suffering.

During this phase, a person should embrace spiritual formation, sacramental worship, dedicated study, and renewal of the mind.

Exit

The person starts to see light at the end of the tunnel once they experience a deeper spiritual surrender to Jesus Christ. I dedicate an entire chapter to this section of the Woods because it's a critical shift in the process of deliverance that must be understood in depth.

Over time, once they are walking with the Lord and consistently engaging in the sacraments, there is usually a turning point that opens the person's heart to deeper levels of healing and deliverance.

The World

After a period of deliverance, perseverance, and learning to walk with the Lord, God will remove the person's training wheels.

The person will exit the Woods and re-enter society, taking with them all they've learned.

Often they will experience a level of persecution from anti-Christian sources as well as those unfamiliar with the nuances of liberation from the occult. Christians and non-Christians alike might discredit or undermine an ex-occultist's experiences if they themselves are unfamiliar with the deeper realities of spiritual warfare.

Re-entering society after liberation from the occult takes time. Triggers will remind them of occult trauma and deliverance trauma. They will have to learn how to function in society with their new identity in Christ. This can be clunky, awkward, and anxiety-inducing.

The person begins to engage in social relationships in a larger way. This brings new opportunities for growth and continued surrender to the sanctification process through the Holy Spirit.

The Calling

At some point, the Lord calls the person to use their God-given gifts to build up His Kingdom.

The person by now is spiritually formed, freed of occult bondage, and has a Christian worldview.

Often the Lord will redeem the occult sins of the past to utilize the person to minister to others in the Body of Christ in some way.

To help you understand how this plays out in someone's life, in the next chapter we'll meet Noelle.

2

Occult Deliverance through Radical Surrender

Noelle's story encapsulates the heart of each of the aspects of the deliverance roadmap. Her testimony provides clear examples of the mechanisms that Satan uses to draw people into occult bondage, and describes the detailed process she went through on the path to freedom.

Noelle, a wife and mother of two, lives in Germany and has a tremendous passion for the Lord. She has a background in mental healthcare and shares insights on Christian self-care through blogging. My favorite part of watching Noelle's testimony unfold was seeing how powerfully the Holy Spirit gave her the supernatural grace to traverse this journey as the only Christian in her family, isolated from any local help. By the power of God working in her, she persevered and stayed the course faithfully, with conviction and strength amid severe bouts of demonic vexation and obsession. Praise be to God for her deliverance!

Noelle's Story

Gateway Factors

Growing up in Germany, I experienced a tremendous amount of isolation, with no spiritual guidance, and I turned to escapism to try to get away from my reality and the emptiness I felt. This played a huge role in me eventually getting involved in occult practices and ending up in spiritual bondage.

My parents got divorced shortly after my birth, so I grew up in two households. Every weekend I stayed at my father's. He had been an anarchist, and then became fully conformed to the world. He did his best to love us, but with poor guidance and no rules. Every other weekend, I stayed with my mother, who had remarried. I was scared of my stepfather due to his coldhearted, aggressive parenting, which ended in physical violence more than once.

Because I did not feel welcome in either home, I did my own thing at an early age and felt like I could rely only on myself. I had so many questions, and I always had a feeling there was more to life. I knew there must be something behind all that is seen. I was fascinated with the unexplained and the mystique of it. But there was no one I could ask about these things. Due to this intense feeling of being lost, I struggled with anxiety and depression as a teenager. I ran away a lot and had a constant desire to flee. I didn't know who I was, and I had no guidance or direction. I tried to solve this identity crisis with escapism and drug abuse.

Occult Anchoring

When I was twelve or thirteen, I discovered some books by Carl Jung. Jung was an occultist who sounded wise. He seemed to teach that there was something beyond the physical and that one had to be initiated into the secret things of life. This aligned with my previous inclinations and seemed to confirm what I already suspected to be true.

In my town, there was a lot of controversy around a man named Bill, whom everyone referred to as the madman. When I was fourteen, he brought the teachings of Jung to life for me in a way that made them seem like reality. The madman happened to be my best friend.

Bill was on hallucinogenic drugs most of the time and hung out with his "witch friends."

- He claimed to be able to communicate with animals and plants.

- He claimed to read books that were dangerous and powerful and held hidden knowledge.
- He claimed to be able to decode numbers and the hidden meaning behind them.
- He claimed to be able to predict the future.

All of his claims were fascinating to me, but I believed they were only fantasies. One day, however, my perspective on this completely changed, and I started believing that his claims were true.

On this particular day, we were walking next to a field of horses. Bill told me he could communicate with them through telepathy and make them follow him. Right then, all five horses started running toward us. They stopped right behind Bill and began matching his speed. Whenever he stopped, they stopped. Whenever he walked, they walked.

I had already researched the teachings of Jung a few years prior to this, but Bill seemed to make visible what so far had been only theoretical. He functioned like a bridge into reality for me.

I embraced multiple lies through this:

- I have to be in another state of consciousness to have access to what is unseen.
- Once I have access to this other realm, I will have special power and hidden knowledge.
- Only special gifted people — the chosen, the initiated — are able to access this realm, evolve higher, and see the unseen.
- I tried to communicate with the same horses the next time I walked by that field to see if I also had these special gifts. It didn't work.

Occult Snapping

When I was sixteen, my parents sent me to some relatives in Canada for one year, hoping this would stop me from using drugs. My feelings around this were conflicted. I was happy to be on my own, but I felt discarded and abandoned. Bill and I kept in touch through Internet messaging, and increasingly our conversations became very weird. It was as though another "realm" had been unlocked, and I could telepathically communicate with him. I experienced sleep paralysis and nightmares more frequently, but I thought it was part of my "initiation."

One of the family members I was staying with gave me a book called *Conversations with God* by Neal Donald Walsch, a New Age author who claims to channel God. Reading that book, the anchor was definitively set. Up to that point, I thought the new reality I was accessing wasn't widely known but was just something between me, my best friend, and some weirdos and herb witches. When I realized there was more to it, more to uncover and learn, I was hooked, instantly addicted.

Down the Rabbit Hole

After reading books two and three of the *Conversations with God* series, I adopted all the beliefs propounded as my own. I could paraphrase them in my sleep.

- All is one and all is love.
- God is love and can be channeled by everybody.
- There is no right and wrong.
- Karmic reincarnation is the circle of life.
- Everything happens for a reason.
- Humans have unlimited potential.
- There is life on other planets.
- Quantum physics and energy are the secrets of the universe.

The books frequently spoke of the law of attraction and manifestation. I felt enlightened enough to try some of the practices recommended by the author. I started with meditation, and after a while, I experimented with tarot cards and crystals.

For the next seven years, I continued to incorporate New Age beliefs into my life. After my first miscarriage, I got hyper-focused on the occult and trying to manifest my reality. I bought into the lie that I wasn't enough, that there was something wrong with me I needed to fix. I believed I wasn't high-vibrational enough, not enlightened enough, to deserve the experience of being a mother. I thought my soul needed to heal first. This led me deeply into the divine feminine deception and "womb healing." Eventually, I became a yoga teacher to focus on what I perceived to be spiritual growth and help my soul evolve so I could achieve my goals.

Shiny Veneer

After another miscarriage I was devastated, because I thought I had finally evolved enough to manifest my dreams. I booked a theta healing session, thinking this would be my last chance. The medium promised that my child would be born soon, that the baby would be a girl, and that she was already waiting for me to be healed so she could finally come.

The practitioner "recoded" (with witchcraft and spells) my subconscious beliefs so I felt worthy of conceiving. Two cycles later, I was pregnant with a baby girl. I thought I was now finally enlightened and ready to manifest everything. This felt like my big breakthrough. I had waited so long! Little did I realize that it was another huge anchor for me to continue the occult journey. I also believed I could be of value to others and help them unlock their full potential. This led me to do tarot readings for people. I began having visions for them, tapping into their energy field to communicate with and channel their higher selves. Friends sought my advice often, and what I revealed always seemed to touch them. This fueled my pride and self-esteem.

However, this New Age journey never made me truly happy. It always seemed like the snake biting his own tail. The addiction, false promises, and breakthroughs kept me going. The New Age was my whole identity. There was nothing else I was interested in. I was trapped.

"Gig Is Up" Moment

It is God who delivers.

Early on in my second pregnancy, I believed it was important for me to be in contact with my unborn son. He told me where and how he wanted to be born, so I prepared for an unassisted home birth.

This also lined up with my conspiracy and feminist views on how the birthing industry and medical system worked. I saw them as enemies, suppressing women and their powers.

To prepare for childbirth, I wanted to check in with what I believed so I could spot any fear or beliefs that might hinder a good birth experience. I wrote down everything I thought were my beliefs and values. I was satisfied and proud of myself for repeating what I had learned from many gurus.

But suddenly I looked at it again with different eyes. I thought, *Wait a second. There* is *right and wrong! There* is *a natural law. Not everything is "love and good." Where are my thoughts actually coming from? Who is the narrator of those beliefs?*

This was the first time I had questioned anything in a decade. I researched the New Age and was shocked. I came across terms like *satanic deception*. I threw out everything I thought was New Age, not fully knowing why. I was still far from Christ. I just knew that evil was not what I wanted. I stopped any practices I could identify as evil, such as tarot cards, crystals, or meditating with Buddha statues.

I didn't realize it wasn't simply the objects that were problematic; it was also me and my continued interaction with the demonic. Since the "spiritual realm" was so real for me, I thought I could still channel my son and my higher self. I thought this could never be evil, since it was me and my baby boy.

It was truly a battle between the Holy Spirit revealing the truth and demonic strongholds blinding me.

During labor, I was by myself in the bathroom. I lost time and any connection to reality. I spoke in demonic tongues and didn't seem to be in my own body. I didn't even call for my husband to come into the bathroom when I felt the baby coming.

Shortly after our baby's head crowned, my husband suddenly came into the bathroom. Later he told me he just knew he had to come at that moment. I believe this was one of many interventions by God. This also woke me up from my trancelike state.

At that point, our son's shoulder got stuck. After another contraction, we knew this was not okay. I cried out to God to save his life. Immediately, I knew I had to turn around — and he was born healthy! God literally delivered my son, which was also the beginning of my occult deliverance. He was born on the day that I was born again.

The In-Between

I would describe the "In-Between" as being stuck in the darkness of depression and hopelessness due to my new addiction to conspiracy theories.

After the birth I felt shattered that I had risked my son's life. I did not want anything to do with the "spiritual" any longer. The whole experience severely traumatized me. But I wanted to find God. I still didn't know He was a personal God. I felt the Bible was surely not the place to turn for me. Because I was already interested in conspiracy theories, I was convinced that "truth seekers" would show me the truth.

It didn't take long until life had no meaning anymore. In the New Age deception, there was at least the (false) hope of being "saved" out of this tragic world once I was enlightened enough. But now I was stuck here on this planet forever until death, and then what? Nothing. How depressing. The New Age has been called "the false light," and that's exactly how I felt whenever I slid back into meditation. I knew the spark of light I felt was false.

My new hobby was watching conspiracy media on YouTube that exposed satanic agendas. And then, one day, one video finally brought Jesus into the picture. It contained horrible theology and a deep conspiracy mindset, but while watching that video, a lightning strike went through me. I suddenly knew in every cell of my body that Jesus is the truth I had been looking for all my life. I felt an instant relief from the sense of restlessness, hopelessness, and being lost. It was like finally coming home.

I started to research the demonic, spiritual warfare, and the Catholic Church. I binge-watched YouTube videos on Catholic theology and Jesus Christ.

Colossians One Moment

Because of my interest in spiritual warfare topics, I found Teresa's YouTube channel and watched a video where she was sharing her own testimony. My jaw dropped. I thought, *Wait, this happens to other people leaving the New Age?*

At that moment I knew it wasn't enough to just watch videos on Christianity.

This wasn't just another topic I was interested in; it wasn't another spirituality I was researching. I knew I had to become a Christian, but I had no idea what a Christian life looked like or what this meant. I messaged Teresa to seek help. She was just in the midst of creating a program that would help ex-occultists reform their worldviews and become Christians. This was exactly what I was looking for! I was committed to it from day one. I trusted Teresa and her guidance.

Enter: The Woods

I entered "the Woods" as the program started. Spiritual warfare increased as I went through it. I experienced:

- Physical manifestation in the form of ceiling lights changing colors while Teresa was praying with me via Zoom

- Vexation in the form of bruises on my legs and arms when I removed occult items from my house
- Increased nightmares
- Feelings of being heavily oppressed and weighed down
- Mood swings and increased anger, rage, sudden sadness, and depression
- Increased moments of dissociation
- Intrusive thoughts of self-hatred and condemnation
- Almost passing out during Mass, not being able to make the Sign of the Cross
- Inability to pray or read the Word from time to time

Outside of the close group of the women in the program, I was very isolated. There was nobody I could talk to at home, no friends or family members. It was painful, but looking back, it formed my relationship with Jesus Christ in a way that I now see as a blessing.

Even though the enemy's attacks increased, through leaning into my walk with Christ I also experienced floods of heartfelt contrition along with moments of weeping on the floor in repentance and begging for forgiveness. While I felt the presence of the enemy more strongly, I also felt increased intimacy with God. Every attack by the enemy made me run into the arms of Jesus even faster.

I adopted the following things from the program into my own life:

- Daily Bible reading and prayer
- Studying theology
- Closing the door to friends who were still into New Age practices and ideas
- Practicing frequent examination of conscience
- Dismantling occult anchors (there was no way I could have done this without Teresa's continuous help)
- Listening to and singing worship music

I found a parish where I could attend weekly Mass and had my children baptized.

Exit: The Woods

When in Rome …

I was confirmed in the Catholic Church exactly one year from the point when my Christian journey started. After finally being able to receive Holy Communion, I felt a new sense of peace and freedom. Demonic vexation and obsession slowly but surely decreased the more I leaned into my faith. This took time.

After months of consistent spiritual disciplines, I traveled to Rome. Small layers of deliverance seemed to happen daily toward the end of my deliverance process. I was able to go to Sunday Mass, where I met a priest who educated Christians about the occult and wanted to help people like me. I went to Confession with him the next day, which felt like yet another layer of deliverance. The most important advice he gave me is that healing takes time and starts with awareness — not only healing from my general trauma and emotional wounds, but also recovering from the occult more generally.

In order for me to finally be set free, the biggest thing was a new level of surrender to Jesus in a way that I hadn't experienced before. I knew I needed to trust in Jesus, but the next level was being okay with whatever God had in store for me. As the Holy Spirit entered into me in a deeper way, I dismantled my final "big boss anchor," and the Holy Spirit healed me from the womb trauma, miscarriages, and idolization of family. I started to truly embrace my identity in Christ. I could see myself only in Christ, apart from my worldly desires and identities. I finally, truly felt like I could trust in Jesus, and the oppression of the occult bonds finally completely lifted.

The World

The first few weeks after my deliverance, I felt like I was in a bubble of grace surrounded by a bed of roses. Everything felt good and joyful. But slowly I came out of that bubble and realized the kind of sin and suffering I still had to deal with now that the demonic noise had quieted down.

I decided to go to therapy to deal with the depression I'd had since my teenage years. I found a therapist who did not utilize any occult practices. I learned a lot in the first four sessions with her, but I quit due to her anti-Christian and abortionist mindset.

Other than working on my mental health, I am still trying to answer some basic questions:

- What do I want to do to support our family financially?
- Do I want a hobby?
- What can I do for joy?
- Which friends do I still have?

After being delivered and experiencing the Lord's Divine Mercy, I don't want to make any decision that is outside of His will. Sometimes I'm scared to do anything. I have to learn to be in prayer, to listen to God, but also to not be in freeze mode. There are many things I am still learning, and every season has its uniqueness and opportunity to get to know the Lord more closely.

The Calling

A month after deliverance, the Lord blessed me with a new life! Being pregnant again, the one clear ministry call for me right now is to be a mother and wife.

After going through Teresa's program, I had the chance to write some articles on *Spirit Sanctified,* a blog that educates Christians on spiritual warfare and focuses on discussing occult bondage and deliverance. I feel a desire to continue to share about the occult and deliverance in hopes that it will be helpful to other lost souls like me.

I used to be an occupational therapist, passionately working with people that were forgotten by society, not seen, and often in great suffering and isolation. I believe that some of these homeless and severely mentally ill individuals are also suffering under some form of occult affliction. I wonder if God will use my newfound awareness to better serve in this ministry of serving the outcast and lost.

Intercessory Prayer. I know I am called to intercede for others going through hardship. The impact of prayer from other Christians during one of the most difficult and confusing times of my life cannot be overstated. It changed me. I was able to strongly see the difference between the self-centeredness of New Age worldviews and the self-sacrifice and love of my Christian community, even across the world. Ever since I experienced that for myself, anytime I see anyone in need, I pray for them.

Noelle's Advice

Deliverance should be the top priority. Not because it serves the self and not because spiritual oppression is annoying. Deliverance should be the top priority because any remaining stronghold ultimately *will* pull you backward and cause hurt and separation in your relationship with God.

Persevere, especially when it comes to trusting God and His timing. Deliverance can be frustrating sometimes. At times you may feel like nothing is happening and you will be in this state forever. Shifting a worldview and renewing your mind take time. It's a process, and every little step of the way is important. You need time to reflect and adapt to new ways of perceiving life and God. Looking back on the times when I struggled the most, the times when I just wanted to be done, I see now that those were the times I grew the most spiritually. How and when God delivers you is ultimately up to him, and you have to surrender to and trust in His plan.

Don't be afraid to close doors. Sometimes we are called to close doors, especially with people involved in the occult. This might mean breaking up very close relationships, which can be painful and scary. God is faithful. He reconciles. Maybe there is an old friendship that God wants you to re-engage in. Maybe you will find new Christian friends. In most cases, this means growing in your relationship with God and cutting out distractions to be with Him.

Engage in the sacraments. Deliverance and coming into the fullness of the faith looks different for everybody. However, I not only learned theoretically about the importance of the sacraments while going through deliverance — I also experienced it, especially receiving the Eucharist and the sacrament of Reconciliation (which is a sacrament of healing). After receiving the Eucharist, I was convicted of my sin, especially occult sin, more than once, which allowed me to look at it more deeply and eventually break down more strongholds to partake in the renewal of the mind. After receiving absolution for my occult sins, great chains were broken and huge weights were lifted off of my shoulders. To be reconciled to God after such severe sin is very healing!

Do not isolate and walk this path alone! Having a close mentor and friend on this journey was probably the best thing that could have happened to me. Without this, I don't think I would have been able to lean into sound theology and a disciplined spiritual formation, nor would I have been able to spot a stronghold or dismantle one. Of course, God is sovereign, and He finds unimaginable ways to renew our minds and hearts, and reading His Word convicted me multiple times. However, we are called to disciple one another, pray for one another, and tell a brother or sister in Christ when they are on the wrong path. Why go it alone when we have the Body of Christ?

3

Important Terminology

Before we delve deeply into each facet of the deliverance roadmap, it's helpful to understand the various terms associated with the occult and deliverance.

> **Inspiration**: To discern is to understand and decide on a course of action regarding inspirations that influence our thoughts, words, and deeds either toward God to heaven or away from Him to hell. (Dan Burke)[4]

An inspiration yields one of two results: (1) **consolation**, which draws our hearts toward God and fills us with a sense of peace and joy, in spite of our circumstances; and (2) **desolation**, losing a sense of God's presence in the world.

An inspiration comes from one of three places: you yourself (your values, thoughts, beliefs, attitudes, feelings, behaviors, actions, habits); God's angels; or Satan's demons. Human inspiration can cause both consolation and desolation; the angels give us consolation, and the demons cause desolation, leading to sin and the destruction of our souls.

[4] Dan Burke, "Test Every Spirit: How We Begin Our Path to Discernment," February 25, 2022, *Catholic Exchange*, https://catholicexchange.com/test-every-spirit-how-we-begin-our-path-to-discernment/.

The Occult

The occult is a belief system centered upon revealing hidden knowledge and harnessing hidden power through mental and physical ritualistic practices fueled by satanic signs and wonders.

- **Occult**: hidden or concealed
- **Ritual**: matter plus form plus intention

Satan draws people into the occult by using two interlaced systems that interact with each other.

- **Light occult**: the deceptive shiny thing on the surface ("Satan disguises himself as an angel of light")
- **Dark occult**: the underlying dark occulted, or hidden, reality

The occult comprises many kinds of belief systems: New Age spirituality, "spiritual but not religious," neopaganism, and shamanism, to name but a few. The practitioners of these belief systems would never classify their beliefs as occult, but that is exactly how the occult works. Most people functioning inside the occult do not recognize the root of their practices as such. If they do, they might call themselves a "white witch" or a "light occultist." Little do these practitioners understand that the light and dark occult are two halves of the same system, and both reside in the kingdom of Satan.

The New Age

The New Age is an occult belief system that fuels a narcissistic approach to practical living, in which the practitioner integrates a personal selection of occult modalities to serve the self. The New Age promotes the lie that physical and mental practices yielding positive feelings and thoughts are the same as spiritual growth.

The ultimate goal of the New Age practitioner is to actualize the self and maximize human potential. This belief system falsely presents mental and physical improvement as spiritual salvation.

- The New Age is a conglomeration of beliefs that center around perception, experience, and the self.
- New Age beliefs promote the lie that mental, emotional, and physical practices are actually "spiritual" and lead to "spiritual advancement," "enlightenment," or "achieving a higher vibrational state."
- Most New Age beliefs center around the idea that the Earth is moving into a New Age when humans will become more consciously aware and gain enhanced physical, emotional, and mental abilities.
- Most New Agers don't believe in a personal God. They believe that all is divine and all is experience and perception.

Note: I dislike the term *New Age spirituality* because the New Age itself is not spiritual. It falsely claims that the mental and physical make you spiritually evolved. True spirituality is only unlocked through the Blood of Christ and by entering the Kingdom of God and receiving the Holy Spirit. Any other belief systems are fraternization with the demonic. That's why we should not call the New Age a "spirituality." Classifying it as such recognizes that it's a way to save the soul. And it's not — it's the way to the soul's destruction. It truly is an occult belief system.

You might know one of these New Age archetypes:

- Universalist Eugene — "I believe that divinity is within all things and people. All is 'God' experiencing itself. You are god! There is one universal truth in all belief systems."
- Postmodernist Penny — "There is no ultimate truth! All is relative and based on perception. I have 'my' truth. You have 'your' truth. Good luck winning an argument with me."
- Conspiracist Carl — "Everything is a conspiracy. Nothing is true. Everything is a lie. Everyone is evil. We're doomed. I stockpile resources, and you should too."

Enlightenment Tina — "I take on every single practice possible because I feel like it helps me manifest good things into my life and makes me more spiritual. I love New Age modalities."

Here are some common New Age beliefs:

- The self and the other are the same (i.e., oneness).
- Everything is part of an ocean of oneness, an infinite spirit (i.e., holism).
- Humans are gods and divine in essence.
- All is mind. The universe is mental (i.e., mentalism).
- Humans are entering a New Age of higher vibration/integrating energy.
- Humans can manifest reality and attract things to themselves with their thoughts.
- Humans are fundamentally good, and the true self is unlocked from within through emotional healing work.
- People who don't engage in New Age practices have a lower vibration and a lesser ability to be spiritual than New Age practitioners.
- There are many paths to God.
- All paths lead to eternal life.
- Souls reincarnate to learn lessons and evolve spiritually.

Identity Theft Avatars

When you do not hold your identity in Christ, a whole bunch of lies can come in to fill that vacuum. The world and Satan will tell you all kinds of lies about who you really are. I call these "Identity Theft Avatars."

Satan is an identity thief. Satan's primary objective is to obfuscate the truth of who you are, which results in keeping you away from accepting your eternal salvation in Christ. Once that occurs, he knows the gig is up, so he tries exponentially to distract you and get you to hold your identity in something that is perishing, spiritually dead, and not the truth of who you are. This is called *misdirection*.

The New Age offers many Identity Theft Avatars that you can try on like so many hats. Get bored of one identity? Take it off and put something else on. Want more than one? Have as many as you like! The occult programs you to think you always need to do more and be more in order to be spiritually advanced. Instead of anchoring your identity to who you are in Christ, you instead take on identities that lead you to burnout, depression, delusion, despair, distraction, and eventually, perdition.

Many occultists have a list of identifiers that make them feel important and loved. These Identity Theft Avatars include:

- Tarot reader
- Psychic
- Intuitive empath
- Kitchen witch
- Reiki master
- Shamanic healer
- Energy practitioner

It is beyond incredible to watch Jesus break a person free of these fake identities and restore them to their true identity in Christ.

New Age Origins

Where does the New Age come from? Although the New Age espouses to be something new, the origins of this type of belief system go all the way back to the Garden of Eden and Original Sin.

I break down Original Sin into four steps:

1. Satan told Eve a lie, appealing to her pride and encouraging her to establish herself as her own authority.

2. Eve physically interacted with a stimulus that caused physical pleasure, which brought about a (deceptive) physical confirmation of Satan's lie.
3. Satan deceived Eve into believing the lie, enticing her into lustful and prideful thoughts, which produced in her a desire to engage in sin. Eve thought the sin would produce pleasure, wisdom, knowledge, and godliness.
4. Finally, Eve engaged in sin, which separated her from God. This is incredibly revealing about the way Satan deceives humanity into occult bondage. I call this process *occult anchoring,* and that is what the first half of this book is all about. Let's begin.

Part 1

Into Occult Bondage

GATEWAY FACTORS

Historical factors lead toward occult engagement.

›

OCCULT ANCHORING

"Snap" into following Satanic signs and wonders into the occult.

›

DOWN THE RABBIT HOLE

Dive deeper into occult bondage through occult practices.

›

SHINY VENEER

Adopt occult worldviews. Deception is secured.

›

THE GIG IS UP

1+ events destabilize occult worldviews. Take pause.

4

You don't simply end up in occult bondage for no apparent reason. There are many factors that impact the occurrence of this type of spiritual imprisonment. Analyzing your history will usually tell a story about why you chose to lean toward the occult.

Four Gateway Factors

I assess four major sectors when digging through a person's history to determine the factors that drew them into the lie.

1. Family history factors

A person's family history greatly affects their propensity to become involved in the occult. If their parents, siblings, or extended family have occultism in their backgrounds, this is a big gateway factor, because the person grew up around occult worldviews. When a child comes into the world, the parent's worldview creates the environment in which the child experiences reality and interfaces with the world around them. Occult ideation is often imparted to the person, even if subconsciously, with no direct education in the occult by the parent. Family history factors affecting a person's eventual choice to draw into the occult include psychological, mental, physical, and spiritual issues.

2. Childhood factors

If a child is around occultism on a consistent basis, this ideation is imparted and taught, and becomes ingrained into the child's worldview. Often a person who eventually gets wrapped up in the occult has an extensive history of traumatic events that occurred during childhood. Unfortunately, a history of trauma, neglect, and abuse are huge factors in eventual occult involvement. Many of the women I work with who are coming out of occult bondage have some form of childhood sexual abuse in their past. Often the afflicted person experienced trauma consistently over the course of their upbringing.

3. Bridge to the occult

Before the person ends up in the occult, there is usually a period of time where they are living in the world and on the world's terms, rather than for the Lord. The pattern I often see is that the person starts to seek after one or more of the following four things: power, knowledge, comfort, or healing. They become drawn toward occult involvement in an attempt to "solve" an issue or gain something of perceived value in a way that they believe will be a quick fix or easy answer.

4. Character assessment

After a person analyzes their family history factors, childhood factors, and the bridge to the occult, they can usually identify a few character traits that ultimately led to them into occult involvement. Assessing these character traits can help them determine the virtues they should focus on when attempting to rid themselves of occult worldviews.

Anchors

You can think of your sins as anchors that dull your senses spiritually and separate you from the love of God. I define an *anchor* as a doorway for the enemy to gain a foothold for oppression. Simply put, an anchor is a lie believed. I describe two specific types of anchors that hook people and drag them into spiritual bondage: **worldly** and **occult**. Each type of anchor is usually accompanied by one or more relevant traumatic experiences. When someone receives the sacraments, particularly private (auricular) Confession, and engages regularly in spiritual disciplines such as prayer and fasting, these anchors are removed, and the enemy no longer has a foothold to oppress and bully the afflicted individual.

Worldly Anchors

> Do not love the world or the things of the world. If anyone loves the world, the love of the Father is not in him. For all that is in the world, sensual lust, enticement for the eyes, and a pretentious life, is not from the Father but is from the world. Yet the world and its enticement are passing away. But whoever does the will of God remains forever. (1 John 2:15–17)

Worldly anchors are things of this world we become fixated on and idolize above God. Worldly anchors can include personal growth, societal contribution, career, finances, health, social life, romance, fun, and people. If you begin to idolize a worldly anchor, you can become desperate or obsessive about that concept or goal, and this can lead to the attempt to control, manipulate, or gain power, knowledge, comfort, or healing by means of the occult.

Some worldly anchors are more prone to lead you into the occult than others. Some of the main culprits are seeking healing, money, knowledge of the future, power, or a desire to connect with a loved one who has passed away. If you are not protected by a Christian outlook, you can get caught up in the occult as a means to fulfill a desire that stemmed from a worldly anchor.

Occult Anchors

An occult anchor is an occult practice or belief. After observing my own experience with occult bondage and deliverance and then entering into ministry to help liberate others from occult influence, I began to notice a pattern. In talking with hundreds of people around the world, I found that Satan uses the same system to lead and trap people into this type of bondage. I compiled this into a framework and coined it occult anchoring. We cover this extensively in chapter 5.

Relevant Traumatic Experiences

The basis of any anchor is usually a traumatic event or series of traumatic events.

> My wanderings you have noted; are my tears not stored in your flask, recorded in your book? (Ps. 56:9)

After a person undergoes trauma, they can suffer a loss of identity or a feeling of being trapped. Unfortunately, Satan can swoop in with a lie about their identity associated with the traumatic event. Sometimes a person will accept that lie and turn away from God, seeking the world or other faulty forms of healing that don't offer true healing and damage the soul. Conversely, they might recognize the lie as such and turn toward God to heal the trauma and to speak truth into their life so they can release the lie and believe the truth.

Big traumas include sexual abuse, loss of a loved one, domestic violence, child abuse, illness, or witnessing death. Smaller traumas include divorce, financial insecurity, bullying, a parent with a mental illness, or an interpersonal conflict.

Sometimes trauma causes a person to dissociate or detach themselves from reality.

> There are many life experiences that may be associated with intense dissociation, such as psychological trauma, substance use, head injuries, and/or experiencing intense emotions like overwhelming fear or anger.[5]

Some people with a history of complex trauma describe commonly dissociating from their surroundings during times of stress.

> When a person feels trapped in a triggering situation, they may use dissociation to escape the overwhelming emotions they are feeling in the current moment. A variety of dissociative symptoms show up, including depersonalization and derealization.[6]

Trauma can be a gateway factor into the occult because the ability to dissociate is utilized heavily in multiple occult practices, such as

5 "Dissociation and Trauma in Young People," Orygen: The National Centre of Excellence in Youth Mental Health, December 31, 2018, https://www.orygen.org.au/Training/Resources/Trauma/Fact-sheets/Dissociation-trauma/Orygen_Dissociation_and_trauma_in_young_people_fac.

6 Andrea Brognano, "Anxiety & Dissociation: How Are They Connected?" *Choosing Therapy*, May 3, 2023, https://www.choosingtherapy.com/anxiety-and-dissociation.

astral projection, certain forms of divination, remote viewing, occult meditations, and channeling.

Some traumatic events cause a person to feel deep despair and divine abandonment. Many times when the Holy Spirit comes into a person and starts to heal them from trauma, a realization washes over the person. The person realizes that Jesus was with them at that moment, that they were not abandoned at all, and that all suffering is recognized and deeply felt by Our Lord.

Cultural Traps

Certain narratives entrenched in modern American culture are particularly damaging and deceiving and can lead people into occult bondage.

I have a formula that goes like this:

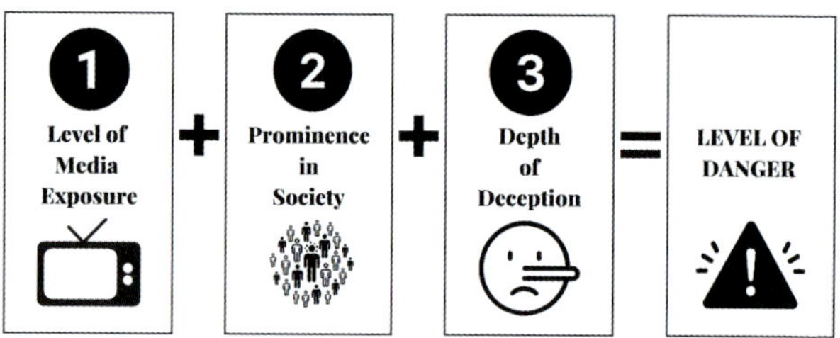

In speaking with people from all over the world who have come out of occult bondage, some cultural narratives keep coming up over and over again. I've compiled a list of the top cultural traps often mentioned by ex-occultists as either leading them into or directly causing them extensive theological distortions and/or spiritual damage.

Gnosticism

Gnosticism, a word that stems from the Greek word *gnosis,* is an ancient heresy that teaches that you can achieve salvation through accessing secret knowledge:

- Humans can unlock wisdom from within.
- Humans can access wisdom apart from their creator.
- Humans are gods, and the body is evil.
- Spiritual/true liberation is achieved through exiting the body.
- Christians are "uninitiated" and ignorant.

Only those enlightened through gnosis are truly saved by the secret information they claim to possess.

Gnosticism is a satanic trap that keeps people locked into seeking mental practices and information that is unspiritual — worldly wisdom that is perishing. Gnostic channeling/meditation is very dangerous. The practice includes the invocation of the demonic. At this point, the demonic can enter into the person. With gnostic channeling, the demon will often give the person information that draws them deeper into occult beliefs and practices.

Eastern Practices

The New Age draws beliefs from many sources, but most teachings are derived from Hinduism and Buddhism. Various beliefs include:

- All is one.
- Oneness is God.
- All is God.
- The world is an illusion.
- Separateness is an illusion.
- Good and evil are the same thing.
- We are all divine.
- God is an impersonal "force" or "energy."

- We seek enlightenment through meditation.
- Reincarnation is true.

We can shorten reincarnation cycles through good works to stop coming to the Earth to work out karma. Our actions in life, good or bad, are tallied up. Countless lives are needed to obtain nirvana or oneness.

New Age gurus often cherry-pick Hindu and Buddhist teachings and offer various meditation techniques that claim to help a person achieve oneness. These techniques amount to a pointless chasing-the-tail game of seeking oneness, with the goalpost constantly moving. These practices and beliefs create cycles of perceived growth that take a person nowhere and lock them into mental and physical practices that are not spiritual.

Human Potential Movement (HPM)

The Human Potential Movement (HPM) fuels the notion that we have a large amount of untapped potential within us, and teaches that harnessing this potential can manifest happiness, creativity, and ultimate dream fulfillment. HPM was built upon the teachings of Abraham Maslow, a humanistic psychologist who taught that humans reach their potential through self-actualization.

Maslow described the height of human potential as peak experiences, or euphoria, and stated that the triggers of these experiences included "art, nature, sex, creative work, music, scientific knowledge, and introspection." Peak experiences center around altered states of consciousness and attempt to evoke euphoria, and truth is defined as one's experience. HPM draws from Hinduism and is often bound up with Transcendental Meditation and psychedelic drugs.

Today, HPM has become normalized in American culture through social media, politics, higher education, mass culture, health and wellness cults, and self-help books.

The Human Potential Movement fuels self-focus and leads its proponents to lean on their human understanding and abilities for spiritual improvement, an effort that is ultimately futile. The Human Potential Movement does not have spiritual answers for the questions of physical, mental, or emotional handicaps or suffering.

Unconventional Health

Many occult practices are based upon alternative healing methods that conflate spiritual healing with physical healing. This can keep us locked into the distortion that physical and mental healing are the same as spiritual healing, which they are not. Only Jesus' Blood offers spiritual healing.

The National Center for Complementary and Integrative Health defines complementary health as "non-mainstream approaches used together with conventional medicine," and it defines alternative health as "non-mainstream approaches used in place of conventional medicine."[7] Overall, these approaches are considered unconventional, and typically have roots beyond the tradition of Western medicine.

Unconventional medicine can be classified into five categories: "whole medical systems, mind-body techniques, biologically based practices, manipulative and body-based therapies, and energy therapies."[8] The systems, beliefs, and approaches explored in uncon-

[7] "Complementary, Alternative, or Integrative Health: What's in a Name?," National Center for Complementary and Integrative Health, U.S. Department of Health and Human Services, September 28, 2021, https://www.nccih.nih.gov/health/complementary-alternative-or-integrative-health-whats-in-a-name.

[8] Denise Millstine, "Types of Complementary and Alternative Medicine," *Merck Manuals*, https://www.merckmanuals.com/home/special-subjects/integrative-complementary-and-alternative-medicine/types-of-complementary-and-alternative-medicine.

ventional health vary in credibility, ranging from providing fairly clear scientific proof to relying on totally unproven and even unfalsifiable claims. Some of these systems have a scientific basis, but can lead one into the occult through idolatry and pride; others have significant overlap with occultists, who mix witchcraft with alternative medicine. You can be led from something non-occultic into forms of witchcraft without even realizing what is happening. Also, many of these beliefs and practices tend to be leveraged in conspiracist circles that point people away from widely accepted science.

While it is generally prudent to approach any material with care, personal research, and from a standpoint of remaining anchored in Christ, there should be a balance in responsible integration of beliefs and practices related to health. That being said, every single one of the five classifications explored in unconventional medicine contains aspects of occultic draw and must be approached with either extreme caution or else not at all. Components of unconventional medicine can easily draw a person directly into the occult.

Here are some examples of ways that each of the five unconventional health systems might lead you astray. Chapter 5 will explain how these systems that seem benign on the surface actually can lead you into the occult.

Whole medical systems

- **Ayurveda** is a form of traditional Indian medicine that claims to promote spiritual healing. This can become a replacement for giving God glory and praise for the healing of our bodies, minds, and spirits. If idolized, it can serve as a false replacement for salvation in Christ, and sanctification by the power of the Holy Spirit.
- **Traditional Chinese medicine** claims to promote spiritual healing. This can become an idol in the same way as ayurveda.

Mind-body techniques

- **Hypnotherapy/hypnosis** can lead to an interest in altered states of consciousness. These can put you in a vulnerable state, in which your human imagination and/or demonic inspirations can lead to occult practices such as gnostic channeling, past life regression, and astral travel.
- **Meditation**, generally speaking, involves breathing exercises and clearing the mind, neither of which is occultic in nature. However, you should approach meditation with caution, as there are types of meditation that involve occult practices.

Biologically based practices

- **Botanical medicine.** There is nothing intrinsically wrong with using plants for medicine. But when used with other forms of unconventional medicine and combined with idolatry, there are definitely cases where a person will begin moving into witchcraft or "hearth magic." Modern occultism often utilizes herbalism, which can sometimes be traced back to an initial interest in biologically based practices. These practices in themselves are not occultic in nature, but the occult often draws from science and the history of these practices.
- **Natural products and supplements.** This one is a bit complicated. Often a person will get into natural products and supplements through consumption of alternative media and conspiracist content. Then, the practices of intaking natural products can turn into idolatrous obsession. This can evolve into paranoia about the world and about things of an "unnatural" origin. The obsession can lead to rapid and greedy consumption of more alternative beliefs, which can turn a person off from anything seemingly "mainstream" or with general authority. Anti-authority worldviews can draw

a person into the occult, because they orient a person toward shucking off any worldview that is seen as mainstream. This attitude leads to interests in deeper conspiracy media, the paranormal, and the occult. (See Conspiracist Worldviews later in this list.)

Manipulative and body-based therapies

- **Naturopathy.** One form of naturopathy is acupuncture, which often is accompanied by a belief in the chakra system, sometimes blended with forms of witchcraft such as crystal healing and energy healing. Acupuncture exposes you to occult terminology and can draw you into occult beliefs and practices. In some cases, occult practices are performed over the person receiving acupuncture.
- **Massage or chiropractic care.** Neither of these practices is occult in nature, but there are occult teachings that surround the training in each of these systems, so if you're seeking massage therapy or chiropractic care, you want to make sure to select a specialist who is not blending in occult practices. Practitioners themselves should take care not to incorporate occultic methods into their practices, and if you are seeking this type of care, make sure to work with a spiritually sound therapist.

Energy therapies

- **Reiki** is a popular modern occult practice that was popularized in the United States in the 1970s when the first reiki clinic opened. Reiki is a form of witchcraft that claims to channel lifeforce energy, invoked through the practitioner and then evoked into the person seeking to receive the healing. This form of witchcraft opens both the practitioner and the person seeking healing to making pacts with demonic spirits, as it is an occult practice involving invocation and evocation.

The Law of Attraction

The Law of Attraction is the New Thought belief that you can use your thoughts to attract positive or negative experiences into your life. By holding a positive or negative thought in your mind, supposedly you will attract or evoke (call forth) a perceived "aligned" experience. In theory, positive thinking attracts positive experiences and negative thinking attracts negative experiences.

The basis of the belief centers upon the idea that people and thoughts are comprised of pure energy — an occultic/esoteric principle — and that through focusing on creating certain thought patterns, you can achieve various goals, mainly the perceived manifestation of health, wealth, or personal relationships. Energy (force, lifeforce, *qi*) in this context is perceived as the impersonal substance of God, which can be channeled into the physical world to imbue the practitioner with power to achieve goals.

Drug Culture

Drugs that cause hallucinations, mind-altering effects, and distortions of reality can lead to occult engagement. Some people become addicted to these experiences because they feel like they are experiencing the world at a higher level or in a deeper dimension. Drug culture encourages escapism through physical objects that alter the mind. Mixing drug culture with New Age beliefs and practices can lead to a bad spiritual situation. First, euphoric experiences and hallucinations mixed with New Age ceremonies and practices can conflate physical and mental experiences with spiritual advancement. Shocking and intense experiences while on drugs can destabilize one's worldview and make one more susceptible to believing in the occult. If one is drawn to go deeper into experimentation with altered states of consciousness, it's a hop, skip, and a jump into gnostic channeling and seances.

Drug culture on its own doesn't equal occult involvement. However, drugs are often used in shamanic and occult ceremonies and can be combined with the evocation and invocation of demonic spirits. Because of the altered states of consciousness experienced while on drugs, the demonic can present in whatever form might strike a person's curiosity, opening them up to making pacts and agreements with the satanic.

I have heard many unfortunate — and frankly, quite scary — firsthand accounts of people who have gone to drug ceremonies only to be met unsuspectingly with all kinds of occult rituals. I've heard stories of spiritual abuse occurring when people were on drugs and in a vulnerable and, at times, incapacitated state. In some situations, occultists come in as a surprise to the attendees and begin to evoke and invoke the demonic. People report having visions of various entities. Sometimes they appear as positive beings; sometimes not. I've heard too many stories of people leaving those places and then having a spiritual issue or being plagued by demons after the fact. These rituals are not to be messed with. It's sad that people get dragged into such situations because of drug culture and then become either fascinated by the occult and drawn into it, or terrified of the demonic because they have a spiritual issue.

Occult rituals aside, drug culture must be approached with extreme caution. A person should have a healthy knowledge of occult red flags to make sure they aren't getting unwittingly looped into occult practices or tricked by the demonic into occult beliefs.

Entertainment Cults

Many New Age and occult beliefs are folded into mass media. These satanic agendas in various forms can be found almost everywhere today. Concerts, conferences, festivals, and parties are used to leverage occultism against masses of people all at once. This evokes experiential fallacies on a mass scale. Entertainment cults induce the destabilization of worldview while providing various euphoric experiences. When multiple people experience something together, it reinforces the belief that the accepted lie is true, leading to the acceptance of lies on a mass scale. Groups then band together in their occult beliefs.

The entertainment industry leverages various media to celebrate occult beliefs and practices. Some of these media include:

- **UFO events.** People come together, enter altered states of consciousness, and attempt to "call down" spiritual forces, extraterrestrials, or other higher-density beings from the universe. This is done, often unintentionally, through the invocation and/or evocation of demonic spirits. When the group sees some phenomenon, they often associate the wonder with something positive instead of demons, drawing them deeper into seeking demonic signs and wonders.
- **Concerts.** Some musicians incorporate occult images and messages that glorify Satan into their concerts. Some actually perform occult rituals on stage. At times a satanic sign or wonder accompanies the ritual and people (especially those who hold a deep level of identity as a fan of the artist) are entranced at once into believing there is some magical significance to the act performed, drawing them toward intrigue in the occult.
- **Music videos.** Some artists incorporate occult imagery into their music videos that glorify satanic tenets and encourage their viewers to engage in the occult. The celebrity factor of an artist can appeal to people who want to be included in the hype. You can often observe these types of people who then jump on social media to glorify and support whichever satanic agendas the artist endorses.

Satanic signs and wonders can accompany these events, especially when invocation or evocation is occurring amid other occult practices. The occult snapping creates reinforcement of the cult walls, leading a person to cut off the world and normal reality, while thinking others are less spiritual or not enlightened.

Attention is often placed on leaders, their message, and the experiences they can provide. Leaders feed off the followers' attention and money. Followers feel a sense of belonging which ends up being empty because the whole thing was a lie in the first place. Feel-good escapism never fully satisfies. This induces a fleeting feeling of the New Age concept of love and light.

Modern Occultism

Occultism is the veiled worship of Satan. As millions of people reject God and move into a state of open rebellion and disobedience, they take on occult practices.

These include, but are not limited to, horoscopes, tarot cards, palm reading, Ouija boards, crystals, seances, shamanism, Reiki, healing modalities, psychics, mediums, spiritism, ESP, remote viewing, and overall, seeking power, knowledge, healing, or comfort by occult means.

Deconstructionism

Deconstructionism is a tactic Satan uses to attack your identity. He doesn't want you to know that you are a child of God, and he certainly doesn't want you to pass through Jesus' Blood into the Kingdom of God. He fuels the agenda of deconstructionism by breaking down every meaning and making you think truth is relative; there is no objective truth. Boundaries are anathema. You should ignore and deny history, along with denying life (which fuels abortion). Ultimately you are led to deny God's plan and design.

All texts are perceived as having subjective meaning, so the lie of deconstructionism asserts that you should just decide from your own human understanding what you choose to believe. This leads to denying Scripture as the Word of God and rebelling against the institution of the Church.

Destructive Feminism

Women, your identity is under attack from all sides. Lies are being thrown at you with respect to your personal, relational, cultural, and spiritual identities.

Prostitution, pornography, abortion, and destructive feminist pop music are increasing in acceptance and prominence in society and further denigrate women's identities. Destructive feminist ideation leads to vainglory, wrath, lust, and greed.

Radical feminism's mission is to radically change all social and economic aspects of society, which proponents believe is completely ruled by men. Radical feminists view the world as foundationally dominated by male supremacists and seek to overcome this oppression by rejecting the idea of a connection between sex and gender, which they claim to be socially constructed.

This perspective leads to misandry, or hatred toward men, establishing women as victims of men regardless of actual circumstances. It develops an attitude of animosity by women toward nearly half of the population.

Proverbs 18:19 states: "A brother offended is more unyielding than a stronghold, such strife is more daunting than castle gates." When pointing fingers and finding reasons to be offended, there is hardly any consciousness left to spend on loving one another. Forgiveness from the past and leaning into how to be like Christ and walk with Him leads to loving thoughts and ways of life. Through creating new patterns of love, humans can break the cycle of imprisonment to negativity and fighting.

Conspiracist Worldviews

One of the main cultural traps I see present in an ex-occultist's testimony directly preceding a fall into the occult is an obsession with the study and consumption of conspiracy media. Over time, these habits lead to a drastic shift in thoughts, attitudes, feelings, and behaviors and to conspiracy worldviews. Conspiracy worldviews are characterized by deep feelings of distrust, fear, and despair that can drag a person into depression, isolation, and even suicidal ideation. These worldviews are deleterious and destructive to the mind and the soul.

It usually starts with the satanic deception that we can receive useful knowledge (knowledge that saves) by digging into conspiracies online. This appeals to our pride and leads us to entertain the idea that we can obtain spiritual favor and demonstrate spiritual advancement by displaying knowledge to the "sleeping masses" or "sheeple." We begin to spread Satan's lies occulted by the shiny veneer that we are doing the world a service by delivering information. Retrieving and disseminating "hidden" knowledge is seen as desirable and advancing to the soul. This is the same appeal from the Garden of Eden.

What is often referred to as "truth seeking" can become a fascination with hidden information, which can lead to occult studies. The appeal to pride here is so powerful because of the human thirst for finding an answer to the evil in the world. We research to feel like we are doing something. This offers a level of comfort and delivers a hit of adrenaline that becomes addictive.

Ultimately, there is comfort in the truth, but conspiracy media does not serve up the truth. Only Jesus does that, because Jesus is the Truth. He is the answer to all the information these "truth seekers" dig through. Information idols can never fill our souls. Next, Satan locks a person's fascination upon fear and horror and draws them into delusion and despair. The conspiracy rabbit hole goes deep.

This red-pilling goes all the way to black-pilling, and then approaches paranoia. They cut themselves off from anyone who doesn't agree with them. They obsess constantly over conspiracy topics and don't want to discuss anything else. This is such a huge cultural trap because it renders the person totally distracted and useless for the building up of the Kingdom. Instead, they are now fixated upon that which is perishing and spiritually dead.

The antidote to this worldview is humility. We must humble ourselves and appreciate that we cannot save the world — Jesus has already done that. We are not called to bear the weight of the world on our shoulders or be afraid about oppression in the world. We must rejoice that Jesus has already borne the weight of the world on his shoulders; we are called to repent and forgive others. Also, we should direct our attention to the call God places on each of us for the work he has called us each to do. We cannot see the plan God has for us if we are fixated upon the world and obsessed with consuming highly addictive conspiracy media.

My Story

Throughout this book, I'll use my own story as a case study, a real-life look at my own journey into and out of occult bondage. In my case, demonic possession did not happen overnight. It was a slow building process, little by little, until I was in way over my head. This is how the enemy works. He brings our souls to a slow boil so we aren't any the wiser that we are being led to perdition.

Family History Factors

1980

My father was an A-10 pilot in the United States Air Force, and my mother was a secretary at the office on base where they were stationed in Suffolk, England. My dad worked at RAF Woodbridge, one of the two twin bases that functioned as headquarters of the 81st Tactical Fighter Wing.

My parents were stationed at RAF Woodbridge in 1980 during a world-renowned UFO sighting that came to be known as the Rendlesham Forest Incident. This incident is one of the most highly documented cases of a UFO sighting, and there is substantial evidence of it from multiple military officials, including tape recordings, government memos, and multiple different eyewitness accounts. The event spanned three days, followed by a government cover-up (of course, that's not how the mainstream media described it).

Childhood factors

In 1992, our family consisted of my mom and dad, my oldest sister (age nine), second-oldest sister (age seven), and me (age five). We had moved to Woodbridge, Virginia, where my dad was a lieutenant colonel serving on the Joint Chiefs of Staff under Colin Powell at the Pentagon.

My mother and father were both devout Roman Catholics, and ancestors on both sides of my family were Roman Catholic basically as far back as we could trace. My sisters and I were raised in a very religious and Spirit-filled home.

Our family regularly attended Mass at Saint Elizabeth Ann Seton Roman Catholic Church in Lake Ridge, Virginia. My parents were very close with one of the parish priests, Father James Bruse. He regularly came to our house and ate dinner with us, and he spent quite a bit of time with both my parents.

At one point, miracles started to occur. Fr. Bruse experienced the stigmata, and when he was in the church, statues of Mary would appear to cry and rosaries began to change colors. Hundreds of parishioners witnessed these occurrences. Miraculous healings happened after Father Bruse prayed over the sick, and many sinners were saved. Knowledge of these miracles was widespread, and Father Bruse was featured in *Time* magazine. These incidents spanned across three years and became widely known as the Seton Miracles.[9]

By 1999, my father had retired from the military, and we had moved to Fort Worth, Texas. My sisters were now sixteen and fourteen, I was twelve, and we now had a little brother, age five. On September 15, 1999, there was a church shooting that left seven dead at a youth rally held at the Wedgwood Baptist Church in our new town.[10]

In the wake of this tragedy, our community witnessed the outpouring of the Holy Spirit, which brought people together to console and pray, across all denominations and faiths. We gathered to hold one another, lament, and call upon the presence of God to heal and guide us through this nightmare. It was a powerful experience for all involved.

Up to this point, I was highly involved in my youth group. I sang in the youth band and spent basically all of my free time between gymnastics, cheerleading, and church activities. I loved the Lord and experienced the Holy Spirit through worship and prayer.

Then, when I was fifteen, I was raped in my own home by an adult male who stole my virginity. This was extremely confusing to me. I didn't feel like I could tell my parents, and the one person I did tell didn't believe me. I felt like I was trapped. Thus began the stirrings of something new in my heart: the desire to flee.

Sitting in the pew at church, waiting my turn for Reconciliation, I repeated what had happened over and over in my head as I prepared

9 Find out more at www.thesetonmiracles.org.

10 Jim Yardley, "Gunman Kills 7 and Himself at Baptist Church in Fort Worth," *New York Times*, September 16, 1999, https://www.nytimes.com/1999/09/16/us/gunman-kills-7-and-himself-at-baptist-church-in-fort-worth.html.

to tell the priest the way in which I felt I had sinned. It was a sin I never thought I would have to confess. That day, something broke inside of me. I felt completely abandoned — both by the Church and by my family. It was all imagined abandonment, but my fifteen-year-old mind didn't know how to contextualize what had happened. I didn't know how to get the help that I needed. That confusion fueled my desire to escape.

I believe Satan used this trauma as a way to enter my life and steal away the next fifteen years. Experiencing this trauma had broken my trust in the Church.

It sounds counterintuitive, but I was confirmed soon after that. I perceived it as a box my parents expected me to check so I could become an "adult in the church." To me, it was a box to be checked for adulthood, which would lead me closer to my goal of moving away from Fort Worth forever.

I graduated high school at age sixteen and went to college. As soon as I was able, I moved out.

Bridge to the Occult

Being in college stripped away my religious upbringing, as I attended a progressive institution. I soon found myself in the throes of the post-modern feminist fiasco that sought to glorify all kinds of flagrant sins and cast off organized religion as an antiquated authoritarian control structure.

I started reading books assigned by teachers and comparing them to the *Catechism of the Catholic Church*, just to become angered at what I perceived to be bigotry. I was taking on the postmodern worldview, unbeknownst to myself, and had started to accept that maybe there really were many paths to God, and maybe it was only because of my particular location on the planet that I had been raised Christian, and maybe Christianity was only a tiny part of a larger whole that encompassed the truth. By the time I was nineteen, I had decided firmly that the Church existed to manipulate, control, and disempower the masses. I threw the *Catechism* at the wall and swore off religion altogether.

Fast-forward to 2014. I lived near the beach in Santa Barbara, California, and worked in the tech industry. I met a Russian physicist who claimed to have "discovered God through science." He was raised an atheist but decided that a Creator God must exist when he began his doctoral studies in nanomicroscopy.

He also was deeply into conspiracy topics, UFOs, pyramids, alternative history, and ancient astronaut theory. Little did I know it then, but I definitely know it now — these topics are absolutely gateways into the occult.

I started researching conspiracy topics and immediately became hooked. Given my background with ufology and spirituality already, I was super interested in the idea that the truth had been hidden from the general public, and I started consuming all kinds of alternative theories about biblical concepts.

This Russian physicist would become my partner for the next couple of years. Not long after we met, we moved to Austin, Texas, and got a place together. The first doorway to the occult was about to open up in my life.

Character Assessment

Before we dive into discussing the first occult doorway in my life, I want to describe the character traits present in my life that led me in that direction. This might help you to identify red flags in yourself or in those you love that might lead toward a propensity for occult engagement.

Certain themes in my life collided to create a prime environment for Satan to gain a foothold. Let me break them down.

Suspicion

I was raised in a family that was already suspicious of authoritarian systems. Because of the Rendlesham Forest Incident and subsequent government cover-up, I was predisposed to harbor a distrust of the media and other institutions that seemed to withhold the truth from the general public.

Curiosity

From a young age, I was passionate about the idea that the truth was hidden and needed to be uncovered. This led me to a keen interest in journalism and motivated me to get a bachelor's degree in that field. I never intended to go into mainstream media — no, I was more interested in seeking, finding, and revealing the truth at all costs. An affinity for alternative media and investigative research was already planted deeply in my soul.

Confusion

Due to my break from religion in college, I distrusted anyone telling me what to believe about spiritual matters. There were influences around me whom I respected, particularly my partner and my father, who were leading me into facets of media that conflicted with the orthodox teachings of the Christian faith. These universalist concepts were presented as complementary instead of oppositional to Christianity.

Spiritual Dissonance

My Christian worldview was shoddy, and I had flighty spiritual formation practices. I no longer read the Bible regularly, nor did I go to church. Yet I was clearly and properly a theist. I would have told you that I believed in God and absolutely had felt the power of the Holy Spirit. I would even have affirmed that Jesus died and rose again. I knew the Nicene Creed and would assert that it was true, although I did not grasp how Jesus dying for my sins affected me directly in my daily life. I would say that the story of Jesus resonated with me because of my upbringing and that other people in the world might resonate with something else. I would say that Jesus Christ was the way to Heaven. I would also say there were truths in many belief systems. So, there were a lot of conflicting beliefs there. I had lots of dissonant thoughts that weren't coherent, and this proved that I hadn't spent a lot of time or effort trying to reconcile my beliefs.

Rebellion

At this time in my life, I was living in rebellion against the Lord. I was actively choosing sin, in part because I questioned the authority of the Bible. When I was in college, an openly homosexual college professor opened up the Bible on the first day of class and started twisting Scripture, claiming that the Church had misinterpreted passages. This, in part, turned me away from the Bible and toward the world and its philosophies.

Unchecked Discernment of Spirits

I have been told by clergy that I have a spiritual gift called discernment of spirits because I've seen and perceived the spiritual realm over the course of my life. But just because we can see something doesn't mean we can discern if it's good or evil. If we have this sensitivity and we aren't walking with the Lord, we don't have any clue what is good or evil. Our ability to know what is of the light is handicapped. Only through the Spirit of God can we see the truth in the spiritual realm. And we only have that Spirit indwelling in us when we are walking in the protection and clarity that Jesus Christ offers. This factor played a huge part in enabling the deception of the enemy against me.

These six factors — suspicion, curiosity, confusion, spiritual dissonance, rebellion, and unchecked discernment of spirits — swelled into a cacophony that catapulted me into a downward spiral and landed me at rock bottom.

In the next chapter, I share the first portal I opened to the enemy that led me into occult bondage.

5

In this chapter, I provide an overview of a method Satan used to anchor me in occult practices. I've taken what I experienced and formed it into a methodological framework that I call *occult anchoring*.

The Framework: Occult Anchoring

After observing my own experience with occult bondage and deliverance and then entering into ministry to help free others from occult influence, I began to notice a pattern. In talking with hundreds of people around the world, I found that Satan uses the same system to lead and trap people into this type of bondage. I compiled this into a framework and coined it *occult anchoring*.

Occult anchoring is the method Satan uses to anchor people in occult bondage. I now teach this methodology to clergy and laypersons worldwide so they can educate others and help them avoid this deceptive and destructive form of spiritual imprisonment.

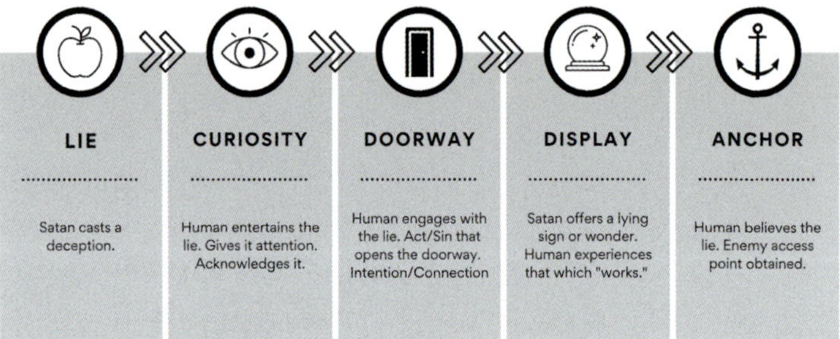

Lie

First, Satan casts a deception. This one is pretty straightforward.

Curiosity

This is the point at which you acknowledge the lie of Satan. You give it attention. There is an element of entertaining the lie, and definitely an air of curiosity. The key here is that you perceive something to be gained from acting on this lie. Your curiosity will generally be directed toward gaining either knowledge, power, or comfort through inadequate means.

Doorway

This is the portal where the lie and the curiosity intersect. This connection involves you actually taking action. You've applied an intention toward the initial lie. This is the act of sin, and the sin itself opens the doorway.

Display

At this point, Satan offers a sign or a wonder to you. This is a lying sign, a display, or an act of Satan that inspires you. It might place you in a trancelike state or a state of awe, because you are seeing something you've never seen before. It's like magic. It's powerful to experience a sign or wonder of Satan. These signs are extremely deceptive and enticing because they lead you to believe the lie.

Anchor

When you believe in a sign or wonder connected with the initial lie, Satan has now gained a warrant to enter through the doorway and gain access to you. You now believe the display and so you incorrectly see that sign as proof that the lie is true. When a belief attaches to a display, this creates an anchor, or means, for a demonic attachment.

Overall, the most important thing to remember is that every single lie of Satan has one overall purpose: to trick you out of and steal the inheritance that God offers you through Jesus Christ.

My Story

Doorways to the occult started to open in my life beginning in 2014 with an openness to reincarnation. Even though I didn't believe in reincarnation yet, the fact that I was willing to consider it was enough for Satan to open a doorway into the occult.

Occult Anchoring: Reincarnation

At the end of 2014 after my parents' divorce, my father started dating a psychologist who practiced past life regression therapy. She claimed to regress patients into past lives as a way to heal trauma through accessing altered states of consciousness. My dad then got interested in reincarnation. He strongly encouraged me to read a book called *Journey of Souls: Case Studies of Life between Lives* by Michael Newton. In this book, Newton describes implementing a hypnosis technique involving regressing patients through a previous death and into the life between lives before they would reincarnate again. The book claims to give readers "a better understanding of the immortality of the human soul."[11]

Reading this book fired me up. I started to get excited about the idea that we could access other realms by going into meditative states. I wondered about the concept of reincarnation. The language in the book was inflating and uplifting, making me revel in what the moment beyond death might actually look like. It was an alternative to the Bible, a source that offered knowledge from a different place — the realm of the mind.

Disclaimer: I love my father with my whole heart. He is an incredible father. Although he introduced me to occult concepts that eventuated in my snapping into occult practices, he also played a big role in my early Christian spiritual formation, which eventually had a positive influence in bringing me back to my Catholic roots. He is now an enormous advocate for the work I am doing to leverage my testimony and experience to help bring people out of the darkness of the occult and into the love of Christ.

The Realm of the Mind

Your mind provides a prime place for Satan to enter into battle. Holy Scripture explicitly says, "Be sober and vigilant. Your opponent the devil is prowling around like a roaring lion looking for [someone] to devour" (1 Pet. 5:8). St. Paul tells us to be sober-*minded*. When we go into a meditative state, our guard is down, and we are more suggestive and receptive to spiritual influences. The mind is a realm where spirits can enter through the senses, offering information, guidance, visions,

[11] Michael Newton, *Journey of Souls: Case Studies of Life between Lives* (Woodbury, MN: Llewellyn Publications, 1995), 106.

and power. But without knowing which spirit is of the dark and which is of the light, how can you test the information?

Well, there are some tells. First, when you are engaging in any practice that seeks to obtain knowledge, power, or comfort apart from God, you are breaking His great commandment: to love Him above all other gods, with all your heart, soul, and mind. You are moving into the realm of idolatry because you're placing something else higher than seeking communion with God. And this opens a doorway that gives license to Satan to advance upon you. Satan is a legalist, and when you are dead in your sins, you are condemned in the law. Satan will be the first to accuse you. If you are not covered in the Blood of Christ, you are a prime target for the enemy's snare.

Reincarnation is a spirituality that circumvents Jesus. The belief that we are immortal without Jesus and have the gift of eternal life without Him denies His salvific work. Jesus is the path; He is the doorway through which we pass, by means of His Cross and Blood, into eternal life.

When a therapist guides a person into a receptive brain-wave state and the person describes past lives, the question becomes, "By what power are they obtaining this information?" This is engaging in an occult practice. It's quite literally attempting to seek out knowledge by intentionally opening your mind to any influence that might decide to come in and communicate with you.

Spirit of Antichrist

Now, why would a good spirit, a spirit under the headship of the Lord, enter into communication with a human to fluff up their pride or give them information that would guide them away from believing in Jesus Christ for salvation? Such a spirit is not of God.

A spirit that seeks to convince you that you receive eternal life through something other than Christ is a spirit that wants you to deny that Christ is God. This spirit is attempting to cut you off from the actual path toward eternal life that is only available through Christ.

> Who is a liar but he that denies that Jesus is the Christ? He is antichrist, that denies the Father and the Son. (1 John 2:22)

Spirits that engage with humanity by appealing to ideas of reincarnation are in league with the antichrist.

Curiosity and Media Enticement

I had zero understanding that Michael Newton's book was drawing me into satanic deception. As I began excitedly reading aloud yet another passage to my partner, he interrupted and declared, "I am a scientist! I am tired of hearing about this book! If it's true, then I will see if it works myself!" And then he jumped on YouTube to find a guided meditation video that would assist him with going into a meditative state and experiencing a past life regression. Even in my pseudo-Christian quasi-agnostic state, I knew this was a really bad idea, and I warned him against it. Something deep down in my soul was stirred, and I knew this was not spiritually advisable.

He did it anyway. He closed his eyes, listened to the track, went into a meditative state, and started to describe a vision from another time, another location on the planet. When he opened his eyes, he ran to the computer and researched the place and the history he had described. At this point, he was fully convinced that past lives were real. Because the information he had channeled matched the reality of that place's history, he believed that what he had experienced was actually a past life.

Past Life Regression: An Occult Anchor

This situation with my partner is an example of occult anchoring. The **lie** of Satan was reincarnation. My partner became interested in the concept and entertained the idea that a person could gain access to a past life through a meditative state. He was **curious** about seeking hidden knowledge. A **doorway** opened when he decided to move forward with actively pursuing the past life regression experiment. He went into a meditative state with the intention to seek and find that knowledge. The **display** occurred when he received visions in his mind of a particular place and time and a certain history of a person. He believed that the visions were actually of him in a past life. This invited Satan to secure the **anchor**. The goal of the initial lie was accomplished. This person now believed in the satanic lie that one could truly obtain and access information from past lives by going into a meditative state and opening the mind to insights from beyond the physical.

In situations like this, the enemy now has an anchor point to the mind through a belief the person has taken on and an associated sin they've committed that corresponds to the belief they've accepted. They start to build up occult worldviews as they continue to engage in occult anchoring. Understanding how this system works is particularly useful when it comes to occult deliverance. When you can identify the initial lie and then the anchor, you can pinpoint the sin associated, renounce the sin (practice) and the lie, and then reform the mind around the truth.

Anchor Clustering and Sinister Agreements

There are always deeper lies attached to what one finds on the surface. On the surface, it appeared that my partner had adopted a belief in reincarnation. However, the more sinister, occulted reality is that he had also accepted an even more dangerous belief that was attached to and clustered with accepting the belief in reincarnation. He had now inadvertently accepted the belief that Jesus Christ is not the only pathway to eternal life.

Let's take a look at what this looks like when mapped onto the occult anchoring process.

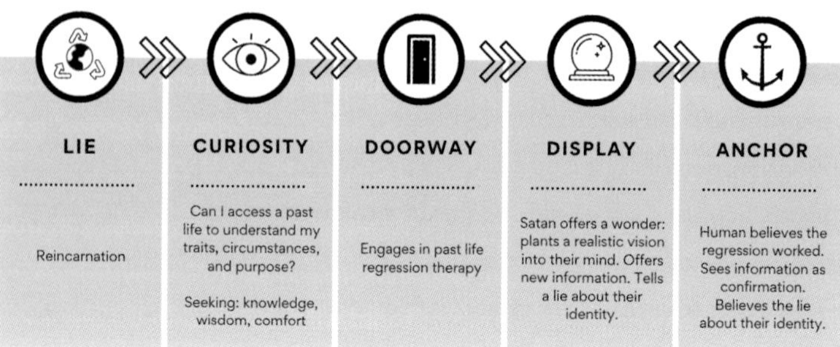

Most people who are overcome with curiosity about past life regression are hoping to understand more about their own current traits, influences, circumstances, and goals. They believe that accessing details from a "past life" can serve to inform their current lives in a way that is beneficial for their spiritual journey.

Another belief system that goes along with this one is the idea that we are subject to a universal karmic order. This means that if we experience some form of suffering in our current life, there is a specific karmic reason for this suffering. So, we seek a past life regression to understand our current situation. In this faulty belief system, we believe such knowledge will help us resolve the karmic debt and return to spiritual homeostasis.

One of the ways Satan and his demons will anchor us is by showing us a false vision that incorrectly explains our pain, trauma, or suffering. The lie is constructed in a way that causes a person to believe something false about oneself or the world that will lead one away from God. Satan offers the lie, and the person contextualizes it in a way that serves their ego. The person literally accepts lies of Satan by affirming whatever these visions provide. These visions can twist up all kinds of things in a person's mind. The person can take on all kinds of incorrect beliefs based on a satanic vision given to them by the enemy.

The act of experiencing a past life regression itself is a breach of trust with God, because we are seeking knowledge, power, comfort, and healing from a source other than God (which is to say, we are participating in idolatry). Thus, we move further away from God.

Consider also the number of anchor points such a person has just created, and so also the number of bricks they've added to the strongholds of lies in their minds. At this point, they are dealing with a cluster of anchors. These things work in concert to create an ideal environment for occult bondage.

6

OCCULT SNAPPING

Worldview Destabilized through Occult Displays.

Occult snapping is the destabilization of one's worldview, which leads a person to "snap" toward a propensity for occult beliefs and practices. Occult snapping occurs at the display point in the occult anchoring process.

Cult Snapping

Ted Patrick, a famous cult deprogrammer, commonly uses the term *cult snapping* to describe a significant change or alteration in a person either going into or coming out of a cult.

> Snapping . . . is a phenomenon that appears to have extreme moments at both ends. A moment of sudden, intense change may occur when a person enters a cult, during lectures, rituals

and physical ordeals. Another change may take place with equal, or even greater, abruptness when the subject is deprogrammed and made to think again.[12]

Occult Snapping

Occult snapping is a term I coined to describe an event that occurs during the occult anchoring process, usually during the phase of the display. When Satan offers a lying sign or wonder to you, this can cause your worldview to be significantly destabilized.

These signs are actually traumatic. You might not identify them as such initially, but when you witness a satanic display, it does a number on your psyche.

You will try to contextualize the occurrence; you will try to assign some significance or meaning to it. Satan offers these signs and wonders specifically to "snap" you into the desire to delve deeper into the occult.

12 Flo Conway and Jim Siegelman, "Snapping," Cult Education Institute, February 18, 2023, https://culteducation.com/group/1280-group/5615-snapping-1a.html.

Occult Bondage Is the Worst Kind

Occult snapping is a highly effective way to draw us hook, line, and sinker into an obsession with occult ideas and practices. Our previous worldview has been rocked, and now we seek more signs and wonders. The display is like a hit of a drug, and once we have one hit, we will want more. The occult is highly addictive, and it is fueled by Satan himself.

Satan absolutely has power and knowledge to offer on this planet. But it is perishing and draws the soul into eternal death. None of the tricks he offers lead to everlasting life. They only serve to draw us deeper into self-absorption, narcissism, obsession with the trivial, preoccupation with the world, and playing with occult powers. His tricks ultimately serve as a distraction to the soul — shiny things to keep us locked in a trance while the life drains from our bodies. We give ourselves over to the darkness with each step.

After occult snapping, we are way past the danger zone. We are already hooked. We will have an overwhelming sense of curiosity, and our worldview is already destabilized, meaning we are looking for answers. We want to know what "works," and we actively seek what something "means."

Each occult mechanism incorporated into the occultist's practice serves as an intermediary between them and God. They end up with a litany of idols.

Occult bondage is the worst kind of bondage. When we invoke (call in) and evoke (call forth) spiritual power, whether or not we realize that it is demonic in nature, we are severing our line of communication with God. Instead of praying to God, our creator, we are giving ourselves over to the elemental powers of darkness on this planet. The heavy dose of satanic signs and wonders makes it extremely difficult for us to humble ourselves; our pride has blinded us to the truth.

Those involved in the occult receive a spirit of delusion because they've refused to love the truth and so be saved. Jesus is the Great Reconciler, but it takes a ton of work for the occult practitioner to get free because of the direct and deep occult sins of intentional idol worship, demonic pacts, and puffing up the self as a god.

Spiritual Warfare and the Mind

We, as humans, were made by God to have three parts: body, soul, and spirit. Our body is our physical body. The soul is made up of our will, values, thoughts, ideas, beliefs, and attitudes. Our souls direct the actions of the body. We are born dead in our spirits, marred by sin and unrighteousness. Because of sin, we are born into a world of death. We are destined to die. We have no ability to do anything good or be righteous in any way. Our spirits are directionless and useless and have no ability to bring us closer to God.

It was only through Jesus Christ, fully God and fully man, living a perfect life, dying on the Cross, defeating the power of sin and death, and rising again that humanity was restored to righteousness. We only obtain that righteousness through faith and Baptism. We accept the salvific power of the Cross and Blood and ask Jesus to come into our hearts, remove our dead hearts of stone, and create in us new, clean hearts. This is when we receive the Holy Spirit. Now we are indwelt by the Holy Spirit. By accepting the purity of God into ourselves, we allow the Holy Spirit to cleanse us and purify our souls. This work is called sanctification.

As this process unfolds, the Holy Spirit comes in and changes us. He shapes our ideas, thoughts, wills, beliefs, and attitudes, and then directs our actions toward the will of God. After receiving the Holy Spirit and yielding to this process through our own choice, our souls and bodies become perfected.

You see, we currently live in a time of imperfection. "For we know partially and we prophesy partially, but when the perfect comes, the partial will pass away" (1 Cor. 13:9–10).

After Jesus rose again and sent out His Spirit to us as a down payment of what is to come, He told us that He would be coming back to fully restore His kingdom. We are currently living in the time in which He is allowing us to choose Him freely, to choose to come into the Kingdom of God. "The Lord is not slow about his promise as some count slowness, but is forbearing toward you, not wishing that any should perish, but that all should reach repentance" (2 Pet. 3:9).

During this time, God has granted Satan and his minions a level of authority to engage with us and tempt us away from God and His promise to us of everlasting life with him. The power of Satan was already defeated through Christ's death and Resurrection, and eventually, Satan's reign over the earth will end when Jesus comes back. For now, we are quite literally living in enemy territory.

Satan wages spiritual war against us largely within the realm of the mind.

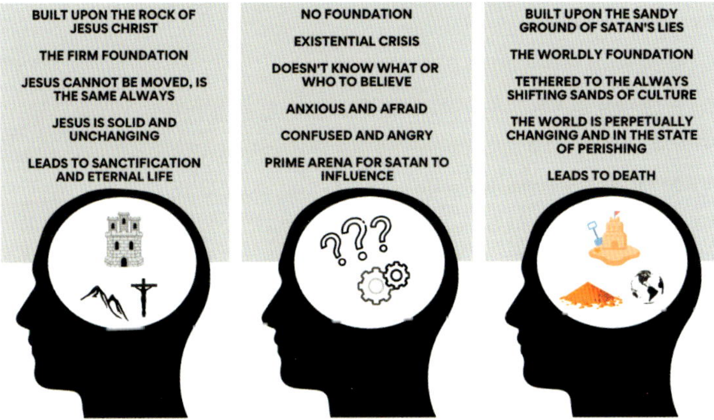

Those on this planet not tethered to Christ are living blindly in a world where Satan is drawing them actively into perdition. Those who realize that the promises of the world are spiritually empty can fall back into worldly pursuits if they don't actively turn toward Christ. Let me put it this way: If you aren't actively running toward Christ, you are a prime target for the schemes of the enemy. If you aren't running toward Christ, running away from the world isn't enough to save your soul.

If you aren't running toward Christ, running away from the world isn't enough to save your soul.

The world is in a state of perishing. "The world passes away, and the lust of it; but he who does the will of God abides for ever" (1 John 2:17). Satan's lies draw a person into traps of thought that keep a person fixated upon things that are actively in the state of perishing. I would strongly suggest reading the book of Wisdom to gain a deeper sense of appreciation for this concept. Wisdom effectively breaks down the idea of idolatry and anchors a person in the realization that it is only through Christ that we can receive access to that which lasts forever.

If you aren't filling your spirit with God, you aren't filling your soul with eternal life. If you aren't feeding upon the spiritual food of Christ, you are perishing and are spiritually dead. Even if you reject the things of the world, if you don't turn toward Christ, you are trapped in trying to do things that don't actually bring you closer to God. And you leave yourself open to the influence of the enemy. If you aren't consuming the spiritual food of Christ and actively choosing Him, it doesn't matter how many times you turn away from the things of the world — you are leaving yourself wide open to be a target of the enemy.

Demonic Strongholds of the Mind

Think about the best possible state of your mind as being fixated upon Christ. You are actively engaging in communion with him and receptive to the purification process by the power of the Holy Spirit. As you engage in this process, the truth pours more and more into your reality. The truth is light, and as you open your heart to the Holy Spirit more, the light gets brighter and brighter. You feel lighter as you accept the truth of Christ. This truth pours into every aspect of your life, and things become more and more vibrant. This happens when you love the Lord your God with all your heart and soul and mind.

Now, conversely, think about the lies of the world. Think about the world as the dominion of Satan, who prowls about seeking to devour souls. Think about each lie of the world as a brick in your mind. Each lie has other lies that are associated with the core lie. When you accept one lie, the other lies around it becomes easier to accept. Each accepted lie adds to the structure of bricks in your mind. By the power of human imagination and encouraged by the lies of Satan, people can begin to accept lies about themselves, the world, and God. Accepting these lies causes the person to turn away from God and turn toward the death-promising practices of this Earth.

Demons run around in groups and are usually affiliated with certain lies. Associated demons flock to certain lies and enhance them through their evil tactics and machinations as they begin to oppress through anchoring. As you build up a belief system of lies, and so accept more and more demonic attachments through the anchoring process, these bricks grow into buildings of lies. Satan and his demons feed upon this belief in lies. These buildings in the mind become demonic strongholds when the enemy takes hold of them. They weigh the mind down and make it more difficult to perceive the truth.

Keep in mind that you can accept the lies of this world and not experience demonic oppression. There's also a difference between accepting lies you create out of your own imagination and accepting a lie that Satan whispers in your ear. Some lies come from a human state of sin, and some are from the enemy. Accepting the lies of Satan or lies of your own imagination doesn't matter, however. Accepting a falsity creates an opportunity because it gives Satan warrant to oppress.

The point I am making is that, regardless of the source of the lie, if you accept a lie, it becomes a doorway for Satan to come in and influence you. Each lie is a brick that creates a foundation a demon can attach to, allowing them to set up shop in your mind. These mental buildings that Satan has influence over are called *demonic strongholds*. Lies take up real estate in your mind.

Let's consider two states of mental focus: one focused on the world and one focused on Christ. What do these two mental states look like?

Everything is about **attention**. The more you focus on the lies of Satan, the more Satan nurtures the fruits you create through that belief: lust, gluttony, fear, sloth, anger, pride, deceit, greed, and envy. Satanic fruits lead to death and fuel destruction. As the enemy anchors into you, over time, he succeeds in building lie after lie in your mind. These lies become demonic strongholds of the mind.

Satan's goal is to get you to take a step away from Jesus Christ and toward his own lying signs and wonders. These things spark excitement in you because his magic trick has worked, but just because something works doesn't mean that it is good for your soul. In fact, seeking entertainment or allure all too often leads to paranormal and occult practices. These things ultimately lead to the destruction of souls.

Occult anchoring is complex, and I don't claim to know all the ins and outs of it. I came up with this structure because I've found it useful to describe a real spiritual phenomenon. But I have no idea why Satan attacks some people harder than others. I don't know why some people progress all the way through to the anchor portion but never seem to show outward evidence that they are under attack by the enemy. Another person might engage with the occult just once and yet the anchor is secured extremely strongly, with grave and detrimental implications.

My Story

Occult Anchoring: Astral Travel

After my partner had experienced past life regression, he emphatically invited me to try it myself. I won't lie — I was curious. I sat down in a chair, put on the headphones, did the breathing exercises, and tried to regress into a "past life." But it didn't work. To my partner's inquiry, I responded honestly, "I think I have too many prayers protecting me."

I remember sitting there with my eyes closed and feeling a thick wall of prayer surrounding me, as though the experience couldn't break through it. I remember thinking that this might sound crazy to some people, but it was as clear as day to me. I knew this to be true. Little did I know that the sinful actions I would take over the course of the next three years would break down and obliterate this surrounding wall of prayer.

After I finished reading the book on reincarnation, I felt a pull to learn more. I had quickly become addicted to the feeling the book had awakened in me, the feeling that there was something more to be experienced than this physical world. I knew through experience that the supernatural was real. There was a tug inside me, beckoning me forward, enticing me to keep going.

One night, I had a spontaneous out-of-body experience. I woke up standing next to my physical body. I was fully conscious; in fact, I felt even more conscious than waking reality. I felt hyper-awake, as though

I had enhanced senses. I looked down and saw a silver cord connecting me to my physical body, which appeared to be asleep in my bed.

In what I learned to call my "soul body" in New Age speak, I traveled around the house and experienced things on a higher, more vibrant level than ever before. I could zoom my vision into objects and see the filaments of fabric connecting each thread of the couch. This, I believe, was a satanic wonder designed to entrap me into the occult practice of astral travel.

Beware of Things That "Work"

The next day, I researched the silver cord and discovered that many people describe this same phenomenon when they have out-of-body experiences. I had never heard of astral travel before, first learning about the term when I did an online search for "silver cord."

I quickly learned that people were able to astral travel at will, which made me super curious to see if I could also learn how to do it on purpose. To me, this was evidence of something that "worked." That, my friends, should have served as a *huge occult red flag*.

When something works, it tends to lead a person forward. I thought, *Well, hey, this works for other people. And the silver cord thing was obviously true for me. So what do I have to lose?* I was curious and wanted to see if astral travel would work for me.

Satan will trick people into adopting occult practices by showing them something that "works."

I taught myself meditation and trained myself to astral travel. My dreams became increasingly vivid. Because astral travel "worked" for me, I believed that it was okay to do. When I was out of body, I would travel around our house and see things I didn't know were there previously. After I would return to my body, I'd go to that part of the house to see if my observations were correct. And they were. This proved to me that I was able to detach my consciousness from my physical body.

Lying Wonders of Satan

Astral travel is a lying wonder, a trick of Satan meant to entice us to develop what we think to be just human abilities. In reality, this is a satanic power designed to boost the ego and engulf the person in the powers of the world and the air, leading them away from true eternal life in Christ.

I didn't realize it, of course, but Satan was playing games with me. He was offering me his power. He knew what I was getting involved in and wanted to give me a good show. He wanted me to continue to research altered states of consciousness, and he used astral projection and astral travel in order for me to dissociate and detach from my body. By doing so, he could make me more available to demonic spirits.

Breaking Down the Anchor

From the concept of reincarnation all the way through to the first anchor that Satan gained on me, the lie was that accessing extraphysical realms through entering meditative states was a reasonable activity. I was curious to see if this was possible. In effect, I was seeking power and knowledge.

The doorway opened when I set the intention to travel outside my body at will and started entering meditative states with the desire to travel into the astral realm. The display — the lying sign or wonder — occurred when Satan gave me his "power of the air" so I could actually leave my body, travel on the earthly plane, and be able to experience magnified senses on the astral or mental plane.

Satan wants us to think this is the "spiritual realm" that proves to us that we are spiritual beings. But it's actually just the mental, or astral, realm. The only true way for humans to engage in spirituality is through Jesus Christ. That is the sole road to the Kingdom of God. The worldly or mental realm is actually Satan's playground. The occult is not the way to the Kingdom of God; it is a trap.

Notice how inflating the entire process is. Satan lured me into further curiosity by showing me his wonders. It's like watching a magic trick and wanting more. It's a bait and switch. I was looking at the wonder, mesmerized, not realizing that underneath the surface, I was giving up my very soul. One sin of pride at a time, Satan anchored me when I believed the lie. I believed that these practices were okay; in fact, I believed exploring the astral realm was a natural thing to do.

At this point, I started to believe in reincarnation. I thought the more I developed these "natural abilities," the more spiritual I would become and the closer I would get to ascension — i.e., not having to reincarnate here anymore. Reincarnation teaches that once you've "advanced" to a certain level of spirituality, you don't have to keep coming back. You've learned what you needed to learn here and can go on to other, greater things.

Occult Fuel: Isolation and Desire

Soon after this, I experienced a miscarriage. I curled up in the fetal position in my bed and prayed Rosary after Rosary. I was inconsolable. Not much later, we moved across the country to Rhode Island, because my partner wanted to improve his relationship with his family.

We settled in a little house on the ocean, and my partner began traveling to China for long periods of time. I felt extremely isolated, and I began having severe panic attacks, even forgetting where I was at times. Due to my partner's affinity for science, he had me following a strict regimen of charting my cycle so we could conceive. Every month when we didn't succeed, he would tell me it was my body's fault. He put me on medication and made me visit multiple doctors, all the while refusing to get a professional sperm analysis.

At this time in my life, due to my loneliness, the responses of my partner, and the pain of miscarriage, I was desperate to conceive. Soon I basically tripped headfirst into full-blown witchcraft.

7

When attempting to understand the realm of the occult and how Satan operates within this system of deception, it's critical to grasp that much of this spiritual war occurs within the mind. If Satan can get into your head, he can start convincing you of things, and this then turns into physical habits of sin, with serious spiritual implications.

Conflation: Mental and Physical Do Not Equal Spiritual

The occult seeks to conflate mental and spiritual practices with spirituality. The following diagram lays out this aspect of the spiritual war that rages on in earnest, as we wait in hope for the Second Coming of Our Lord.

Satan uses deceptive New Age and universalist teachings to convince us that the realm of the mind is the realm of the spirit. This is

part of the way that Satan traps people in occult bondage. When we accept that occult practices are spiritually beneficial to our progress, we become trapped in loops of sin that we believe to be good for us. In fact, on a certain level, people in occult bondage believe that by engaging in these practices, they are being sanctified. This is another lie of Satan.

The only way for sanctification to occur is by the power of the Holy Spirit. Notice the line on the diagram. It is only through the Blood of Jesus that we enter the Kingdom of God. It is only through the Blood of Jesus that we are freed from sin and can engage in a spiritual life the way God intends for us. Spiritual growth comes through sanctification fueled by the power of the Holy Spirit working in us as we yield to Christ.

> He has delivered us from the dominion of darkness and transferred us to the kingdom of his beloved Son, in whom we have redemption, the forgiveness of sins. (Col. 1:13–14)

We only receive the Holy Spirit inside of us after we are delivered from the dominion of darkness and transferred into the Kingdom of God through the Cross and Blood of Jesus Christ, which results in the forgiveness of sins. After the salvation point, sanctification begins.

Occult Practices Do Not Yield Sanctification

Conversely, Satan can trick us into thinking that the more occult practices we adopt, the more sanctified or spiritually advanced we become. This is the lie that we need to *do* more to become more.

The truth is, it is only by the power of the Holy Spirit that we can be made righteous. Humans do not have the capacity to be righteous, because we are dead in our sins. It is only through the salvific work that Jesus Christ did on the Cross and by the power of His Resurrection that we can enter the Kingdom of God.

Satan does not want us to know this, so he puffs up our egos and tries to convince us that we can be made holy by our own doing. These are actually evil actions that infuriate and repulse the Lord God. God does not wish us to choose things that carry us away from Him, and each occult action breaks trust with God because it leads us to choose knowledge, power, and comfort through the powers of the forces of darkness.

My Story

After my first occult anchor, the next stage of my journey was full-blown occult bondage.

Opening Up Pandora's Box

In August 2015, I began writing my first book, *What Is Magic?* In it, I attempted to capture the musings of a young woman trying to reconcile New Age beliefs with Catholic doctrine. Using a fictional format and writing under a pseudonym, I was basically writing my own testimony.

Little did I know that this book would not only be published under my real name, but I would even gain a little bit of fame in the process.

However, my attempt to reconcile the New Age with Catholicism was really a doomed conquest. Obviously, these two worlds do not reconcile in any way. However, my futile attempt to do so (achieved through a cringeworthy, embarrassing arrogance) was fueled by something specific: *pride.* A book project provided the perfect subconscious excuse to explore the occult. Although throughout the book I indicated moral dissonance around the implications of engagement, I continued to pursue the occult nevertheless.

I was doing the blend with all these things. I was going to church on Sunday, cherry-picking my Bible to fit my narrative, and exploring all kinds of occult practices.

I began by relating concepts from the reincarnation book I had read, and I also told the story of the past life regression my partner went through. Once I started to write, I decided I wanted to explore more deeply all the different aspects of New Age practices, witchcraft, and world religions. It sounds really horrible as I write this now, but that was my bright idea! The investigative researcher in me was on fire and ready to get down to brass tacks.

And so I opened Pandora's box. It wasn't until after I finished writing the book that the occult powers I was attempting to harness would ramp up to a completely different level. (Satan let me believe I was controlling these powers, but that was a ruse to trick me into giving more and more legal license to him.) More about that later. For now, I want to share one of the most important factors of my testimony. I'll describe the strongest anchor (what I call the "big boss" anchor) that Satan gained over me: tarot.

Big Boss Anchor: Tarot Cards

I justified buying a deck of tarot cards by telling myself I just wanted to see if they would work. At this point, I was struggling between the idea of something working and knowing whether or not it was okay to do. I didn't trust anyone; I didn't trust the Bible; I didn't trust any facet of the media. I was confused. Can you picture me fumbling around the occult, trying to figure out what was what and how the various actions impacted my soul? I was trying to uncover what worked, and from there, I was trying to understand what I was coming in contact with. I was asking, "What is this power?" But I'm getting ahead of myself.

When the deck of cards arrived in the mail, I was intrigued. I had no background or experience with tarot. All I knew was that if astral travel was real and worked for me, I wanted to find out what else was out there that I had yet to experience. Whatever that might look like, I was open to it.

So I opened the deck.

A Strange Knowing

That moment had an enormous impact on the next few years of my life. There was an immediate physical, emotional, and mental response — a surge of power that caused me to take a deep breath. I'm serious — I could feel something in the deck that was pulsing into the palm of my hand. I can identify this now as a strong impulse to addiction. This was potentially a demonic spirit of addiction entering me at that point.

One by one, I laid the cards out on the bed. I felt this strange knowing, like a recognition. It was as though I was greeting someone I had a deep connection with from the distant past — like I had suffered amnesia and was re-remembering.

This, too, was likely a satanic deception, a spirit of delusion, to convince me that somehow I had a deep connection to the cards that transcended physical reality.

Occult Modalities: Inversions of Spiritual Gifts

When I experienced the anchor point of reincarnation, I gave a fair amount of consideration to the idea that past lives were real. Now I began to question my immediate connection to the tarot cards through the lens of reincarnation. I thought that maybe I already knew the tarot.

Witches believe that every practitioner has a gift for a certain modality, a belief that encourages the inversion of the gifts of the Holy Spirit. I thought that my "soul recognition" of tarot was based on having developed my connection to this craft in prior lives. Maybe this was my "modality."

Do you see the lexicon I was accepting? Do you see how I placed each little lie of Satan into my collection of data to prove reincarnation? I was seeking confirmation for the reason I was experiencing such a powerful connection to tarot. In reality, this was Satan giving me power, which I then contextualized as one of my human abilities. All of these little lies were being built into strongholds in my mind. These anchor points likely invited spirits of divination and witchcraft to attach themselves to me.

Satanic Downloads of Occult Knowledge

My mind became very flexible and receptive. This receptivity invited Satan to "upload" archetypal information into my mind, which I accepted and continued to receive.

The New Age categorizes this concept by a few different gestalts, including but not limited to:

- the realms of Carl Jung's collective unconsciousness
- the Akashic records
- the field of infinite potentiality
- the universal consciousness
- the quantum field

All of these describe a realm of mind that transcends physical reality and connects us all. This is the realm that psychics claim to access.

My partner and I started doing psychic experiments and found that they, too, worked. I started to believe firmly in the idea that we could receive and access information from this field of energy, and I believed this field held the memories of all humanity, past, present, and future.

I believed that the seventy-eight archetypes of the tarot were embedded deeply into our collective consciousness and I could readily access this information by going into a meditative state while using the cards.

Diving into Tarot Studies

In a week, I had every one of the seventy-eight cards memorized. It happened really fast. It was strange — tarot just seemed to flow so easily for me. As I studied the idea of each card and the archetypes they represented, it was easy for my mind to wrap around each original pattern, each different construct of meaning. As I meditated on the card, I beheld its artistic beauty, and the understanding of its depth would wash over me. It was like an entire construct of meaning was being uploaded into my mind. Maybe part of this was due to my college studies in English literature, but I had an easy time grasping the full breadth of the archetypes, and beyond that, the practice itself. Interpreting spreads (groupings of cards) was second nature to me. I could easily understand the full story the cards were telling me in every exercise I attempted.

And yet, there were some early signs that something sinister was going on. These red flags certainly grabbed my attention, but I cast them off and tucked them away into the back of my mind. The desire to use the cards trumped the idea that this thing could actually be dangerous.

You see, this was a strong pull to pride. To power. To knowledge. To comfort. It was like a spiritual bomb went off in my life because this occult practice was so appealing. And it worked.

Oh, it worked *well.*

Losing Time, Losing Consciousness

Now, you might be thinking this is where things started to get a bit scary. But in my mind, I was only clambering into the shallow end. The first *tell* that the cards might be dangerous happened on day three of using them.

I was doing spread after spread, learning the cards, reading the cards, interpreting them, sitting with them, and contemplating them. And then suddenly, I woke up. I sat up and looked around. The cards were all around me and I was sitting on my bed with the light on. I didn't remember falling asleep, or even feeling tired. The last thing I remembered was being in the middle of a reading. I looked at my phone and realized an hour or so had passed.

This concerned me. This was the beginning of me "losing time." This phenomenon grew as Satan gained more access to me. But I want to note that this was the *first* time it happened. An expert in this sort of thing would interpret this kind of evidence as a *tell* that there was some form of demonic oppression occurring.

Another phenomenon I noticed was that sometimes I could feel the energy in my body being sapped. I would be sitting there reading the tarot, and suddenly I would feel completely drained for a few seconds, as though something was drawing upon my vitality.

Searching information about these phenomena on the Internet didn't quite set my mind at ease. Other tarot readers described both of these experiences and explained them as spirits draining your psychic energy. They said there were vampiric spirits that would sap you and feed off you when you were expending spiritual energy through tarot readings. This was weird to me; at this point I was thinking, *These are just physical cards. Is there anything spiritual actually going on?*

After waking up and not remembering falling asleep, though, I began to think, *Maybe there are evil entities feeding off me because I am engaging in this practice.* That freaked me out. But I didn't really know what to do with this information.

An Appeal to Witchcraft

Another piece of advice from other tarot readers was to visualize and cast a white light of protection around myself beforehand so I would be protected from evil spirits. I was apprehensive about this idea initially, but it ended up being the doorway that softened me to performing witchcraft. Evil spirits want us to believe we have some control over them, but we don't. Satan tricks us by showing us signs and wonders that draw us into darkness and bondage, and because of our pride and curiosity, we keep going. I thought there was light magic and dark magic, but really they are both confined to a single realm: the realm of Satan. When we do one form of magic to protect against another form, we're in a cesspool of occult practices; they are all evil, and they all lead to destruction.

You see, instead of witches correctly identifying that the practices themselves are evil, they believe that tarot is a tool. They don't assert that tarot is either good or evil, but rather it is the intention of the user that determines the nature of the practice. They might compare tarot to a gun — it can be used for a positive or negative outcome. But occult practices merely draw you deeper and deeper into more occult practices. Tarot is against God's law. Practicing tarot leads to taking on even more occult practices. The deceived might think witchcraft will help them, but it only brings them further into bondage.

Seeking Occult Knowledge as a Habit

I started living my life by the cards. Tarot became a friend to me, an advice giver. I initially told myself:

- This is a coaching tool.
- There is nothing magic about tarot.
- Reading tarot is just an exercise I'm using to assess my current situation and then make logical decisions based on what I uncover.

- The cards themselves just serve as prompts for me to consider other sides of an issue. This helps me determine the best outcome going forward.
- I don't consult the cards for divination purposes. I don't claim to see the future. This keeps me in alignment with the religious teachings.
- I'm not divining the future. I'm just considering my present.

How "blend" of me! Amid focusing on worldly desires like conception and trying to tarot my way into viable solutions, my flimsy excuses for the practice eventually gave way to full-blown idolatry.

Was It Really Just a Non-Magical Coaching Tool?

No matter how much I tried to use mental gymnastics to believe my hogwash about tarot cards just being pieces of paper, this state of mind didn't last forever. That's because I actually did begin to access occult knowledge.

At a certain point, tarot began to function in a way that I knew was no longer coming from me. I didn't know that I was playing with demons. But as I started reading tarot for other people, suddenly I could access information which there was no way I could have known. I started to get visions and information and different senses that allowed me to see into the lives of those for whom I read. It was a red flag, but I ignored it and kept going.

Synchronicity: A Tool of Deception

A critical aspect of the occult that is important to grasp is the concept of synchronicity. This is a powerful tool of deception the enemy uses to trip us up and drag us into occult bondage.

Whichever occult practice you engage in, the enemy can offer you his wonders to trick you into believing the lies and fuel your addiction to the practice. Next, you begin to look for a sign that will reinforce, support, or confirm that which you've experienced through the wonder. It works like this:

1. You do a tarot spread that gives you a certain piece of information.
2. You look to the "universe" or the "universal field" to confirm that piece of information.
3. You receive a confirmation, and now you *know* you are on the right path.

This is a tragic practice for a person already playing with demons. You are literally looking out into the world to see anything and everything that will prove what you just witnessed. The word *synchronicity* is New Age jargon for finding such a pattern or confirmation in the world.

Apophenia and Pareidolia

I see two key issues with this. First, we can easily find synchronicity, or a pattern, in something that isn't actually significant in any kind of way. We can be misled into thinking some ultimately inconsequential thing has some sort of deep significance for our lives. We might start following a bunch of insignificant patterns as though this will take us somewhere useful, only to crash and burn as we end up nowhere! Conversely (and possibly to a greater degree of detriment to the person), following the perceived patterns might lead us somewhere great in the world for the time being, and then we think the patterns were actually useful when they weren't.

We can become obsessed with seeking signs and attributing meaning to insignificant things.

A common occult practice is seeking out repeated numbers in clocks and other places such as license plates or symbols. There are alleged meanings attributed to numbers and sequences of numbers. The significance is usually pulled from a smattering of occult typologies including numerology and other mythological or philosophical constructs. All these beliefs are pulled together in a larger loose construct inside modern occultism. Nowadays, there are many websites and apps out there that claim to decipher numerological patterns and symbolic meaning in dreams, spirit animals, and angel numbers. (Angel numbers are repeated numbers that people claim are messages from the angelic realm, the meanings of which are asserted through a conglomeration of occult methodologies.) Some occultists actually live their lives in close adherence to the practice of seeking out, analyzing, and applying occult numerological meanings to the numbers they see, which they call "following synchronicities." The concept of synchronicity is basically a flow by which a person will live their life, zeroing in on numbers they see, assessing the moment those numbers come up, and then making decisions based on those circumstances that arise during the day. These decisions are derived from their perceived meaning, which stems from the interpretations that follow from whichever occult typologies the occultist observes. Synchronicities are essentially pieces of data used to influence a person's decisions in life, and they make the practitioner feel they are in communication with the divine. On the basis of this belief, they think that the decisions they make are in alignment with the highest spiritual realms. Ultimately, it's about control, knowledge, guidance, and comfort.

In general, this phenomenon is called apophenia, which is the tendency to perceive a connection or meaningful pattern between unrelated or random things. A more narrow category of this phenomenon is pareidolia, the tendency to perceive a specific, often meaningful image in a random or ambiguous visual pattern. In short, apophenia is the perception of a meaningful pattern between uncorrelated phenomena, whereas pareidolia is the perception that a vague stimulus is actually something known to the observer.

Here is an example of apophenia that you might see in occult circles. A person is an avid believer in synchronicity and believes in angel numbers. They have been focusing on looking for synchronicities to help them decide whether to buy a car. The person waits for the bus, which is supposed to arrive at 4:30. While waiting, the person sees a license plate that includes the numbers 444. When the bus arrives, it is exactly 4:44. The person believes that this is a message from the universe telling them they should purchase a car. This person assumed that seeing those numbers was actually a communication from the angelic realm — i.e., an angel number. In common occult typologies, the number four often represents stability, so the person attributed an instruction to buy a car to the repeated sequence of fours on the license plate synchronized with the time when the bus arrived. Pareidolia occurs when someone perceives a cloud in the sky (a vague stimulus) to be the shape of a car. In both cases, these might lead a person to think the world is showing them a synchronicity that supports them getting a car. It is a means by which someone leans on their own interpretation of their perception of the world to authorize certain corresponding behaviors.

False Signs and Wonders

The second issue with synchronicity is related to Satan. When we engage in occult activities and seek synchronicities to support or deny certain lines of thinking or paths forward, we are in the midst of a spiritual battle. Satan prowls about this world and will use whatever he can to trick us into making really stupid decisions that take us further away from God. Occult practices themselves appeal to pride and selfishness and lead us into an obsession with the things of the world, whether money, fame, or power. Satan and his demons support these practices by interacting through the means of synchronicity. When a person opens their mind to whatever the world wants to give them, it's an opportunity for Satan to come in.

Without the help of the Holy Spirit, we have no clue how to discern between what is good (of the Lord) and what is bad (of Satan). We're really just leaning on our own understanding.

> Trust in the Lord with all your heart,
> and do not rely on your own insight.
> In all your ways acknowledge him,
> and he will make straight your paths.
> Be not wise in your own eyes;
> fear the Lord, and turn away from evil.
> It will be healing to your flesh
> and refreshment to your bones. (Prov. 3:5–8)

If we live in the world without the help of the Holy Spirit, we are not being sanctified. In truth, we are just following the selfish desires of our own hearts. Looking around the world, open to whatever comes our way, we fall victim to deceptive satanic signs and wonders. In this state of mind, we become a prime target for Satan's deception.

> The coming of the lawless one by the activity of Satan will be with all power and with pretended signs and wonders, and with all wicked deception for those who are to perish, because they refused to love the truth and so be saved. Therefore God sends upon them a strong delusion, to make them believe what is false, so that all may be condemned who did not believe the truth but had pleasure in unrighteousness. (2 Thess. 2:9–12)

Practicing Witchcraft

Soon after adopting the tarot, I took on the practice of witchcraft. Initially, I did this in hopes of protecting myself from the negative experiences associated with tarot practice.

Next, I learned how to spellcast in hopes of successfully conceiving. I learned about moon cycles and moon spellcasting. The whole time, I was thinking back to my childhood, perceiving parallels between what I was learning and what I remembered from my Catholic upbringing. But looking back at these parallels now, I shake my head and think, *What a stretch!*

Example: Witches and Christians both use altars, but their focus is different. While I was able to clearly see that Christians focused on Jesus, whereas witches focused on something else, I still failed to see that witches draw upon satanic powers to influence the world. I was deceived by the idea that *we* can control these forces. Yes, there's an element of control, but it is in the final analysis a lie. It is a ruse. It is Satan giving the practitioner enough power to convince them that they have control. Satan keeps a person hooked by showing them just enough signs and wonders to keep them intrigued so that they'll go deeper and deeper into the occult. Pretty soon, the person is in bondage. Satan now has legal access to them through their sin.

I started using visualization and intention-setting to cast spells, and I even created an altar and started calling upon forces of the earth to assist me with my goals. Mixing elements of witchcraft with prayers to the Trinity convinced me that what I was doing was okay. The first time I ever used an altar, one of the candle flames bent toward me, and I felt the power of a spirit enter what I believed to be the "sacred space" I had cast through my witchcraft. The spirit started communicating with me, and I thought it was the Holy Spirit. It was not the Holy Spirit, though, and it was not a sacred space.

Universal Energy and Occult Healing

I'll just briefly mention the idea that we can "tap into" some form of "universal energy" and channel it in order to heal ourselves and others. This includes reiki, chakra healing, and kundalini awakening, among a multitude of other practices that involve visualization and channeling some form of energy to heal or "level up" spiritually. I learned about and engaged in each of these practices, along with anything else that appealed to my curiosity.

Kundalini Meditation

Kundalini meditation includes breathwork, visualization, and altered states of consciousness. I read multiple warnings in testimonials online that if you didn't "prepare" effectively, you could actually experience a psychotic breakdown. Some people actually have ended up in mental institutions because of the disruption the exercise instigated. Conversely, others describe experiencing euphoria and an increased awareness and perception of reality.

One New Age belief is that if you were one of the unlucky ones who experienced a negative greeting or a psychotic break, it was due to you not being vibrationally ready to receive new, higher-vibration insights. The logic blames the victim for not being spiritually advanced enough to engage, when really they are likely being attacked by demonic forces.

Reiki Certification

I decided to take a course to become certified in reiki. The master practitioner scheduled the initiation ceremony, which would take place over the phone. She explained that she would "impart" the first master reiki symbol to me. She would share it with me so I could then use it to channel the universal power.

I need to offer a note regarding the concept of "universal power." The supernatural refers to power associated directly with God, or phenomena from that which is above nature and of divine origin. Supernatural occurrences are direct encounters with God, the creator of the universe. Examples of supernatural phenomena are miracles performed by God,

God's sanctifying grace imparted in the soul, and workings of the Holy Spirit. An occultist attempting to harness universal power through witchcraft is not supernatural at all, because only God distributes supernatural power. It comes from Him alone.

The preternatural refers to phenomena beyond the natural world but not of divine origin and encompasses occurrences related to both good angels and fallen angels (demons). These phenomena might produce extraordinary effects but are not related to God because they don't originate from God himself. Positive preternatural occurrences might include angelic intervention or apparitions of saints. Negative preternatural occurrences might include demonic influence, oppression, or possession. Satanic signs and wonders, as referred to in scripture, involve negative preternatural phenomena. It's also prudent to mention that negative preternatural forces commonly attempt to deceive by appearing as positive preternatural forces.

In the case of reiki, this practice attempts to evoke or invoke supernatural healing from God through witchcraft, which is ineffective because no human controls God. It instead opens a door to negative preternatural forces.

Before this reiki rite occurred, I did a meditation session by myself. I wanted to focus on purification and receptivity to be able to effectively obtain the universal power through her as a channel. During my meditation, I received the visual image of a symbol, and I drew it on a sheet of paper. I sent the picture to the teacher, and she was flabbergasted. It was the same symbol she was planning on giving me the next day. I don't think she had ever seen anything like that before. I actually freaked her out. I now know that Satan was using this wonder as a sign that we were somehow engaging with the supernatural. It was not a supernatural experience but one with evil preternatural forces. I completed the course and became master reiki certified.

Kundalini Awakening

Next, I prepared for eight months through dedicated daily meditation, one to two hours a day, in order to be ready to attempt a kundalini awakening. After eight months, I went through all of the ritual, the breath work, the visualization, the whole thing. That night, I went to bed and had a really intense dream. In this dream, I was in the spiritual realm. I was being held, suspended, inside a void — what I describe as a "cosmic womb."

It was all darkness, but other than sight, I had my other senses. I could hear all the voices of suffering — all the humans from the past, present, and future, each voice of pain and torment, gathering together in a giant cacophony of suffering. The burden of it was painful. I beheld each voice as a singular eternity of pain, and that multiplied by the millions.

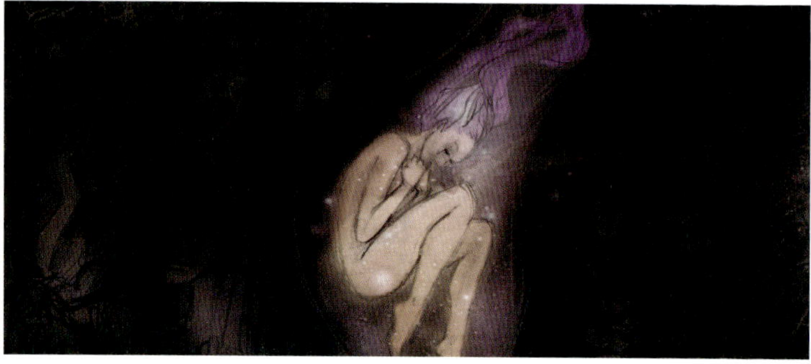

I heard a voice say, "God is stronger than all the pain in the world. God conquered every single moment of suffering, pain, torment, tears, and anger that has ever been, ever is now, and ever will be." This resonated as the truth, but I didn't have even a fragment of understanding of how far from His embrace I was.

The inspiration that came to me from this experience could have come from one of three places:

1. **Human imagination**: Did my own mind create this thought?
2. **Satan and demons**: Were demons trying to drop something that sounded truthful to me so that I would trust the voice and lean into occult practices?
3. **God and the good angels**: Was God breaking through the occult fog?

Likely the inspiration came from one of the first two places, but who knows? Either way, I wish I could have yelled at myself: "Jesus is the Son of God; it is He who redeems all through His death, Resurrection, and Ascension! And He will come again!"

> "He will wipe away every tear from their eyes, and death shall be no more, neither shall there be mourning nor crying nor pain any more, for the former things have passed away."
>
> And he who sat upon the throne said, "Behold, I make all things new." Also he said, "Write this, for these words are trustworthy and true." (Rev. 21:4–5)

Instead, I leaned into the deception that these practices weren't dangerous and misleading. I continued to think I could blend occult practices with an abysmal semblance of Christianity. I deluded myself into thinking I could worship God at church and interact with the same God through tarot cards and witchcraft-fueled altered states of consciousness. Yikes.

The Warning I Ignored

As the book project that I was subconsciously using as an excuse to explore New Age practices came to a close, I spent a week in prayer. I prayed to God, saying, "Okay, God, I just wrote this book. Now what am I supposed to do?"

After a week of deep prayer, the word I got very clearly was, "You need to return to the Catholic Church. Go to the Bible. Look at the evil. Look at the exorcisms." I got this message a few times during prayer. To this day, I don't know why I ignored this directive. I was attending Mass on Sundays, but not regularly, and I didn't seek out spiritual direction. I didn't look deeper at what was right in front of me. I knew in my heart it was the Lord speaking to me, but for some reason, I did not yield.

I wonder how much heartache, pain, and suffering I could have avoided had I heeded that call. It could have absolutely served as a wake-up call that would have put me back on track. But that's not how the story went. Instead, I went deeper into occult practices and eventually embraced a total occult worldview. The shiny veneer had taken over.

8

As you know by now, the occult is a belief system centered upon revealing hidden knowledge and harnessing hidden power through mental and physical ritualistic practices fueled by satanic signs and wonders.

Satan draws people into the occult by the use of two interlaced systems:

1. **Light occult**: the deceptive shiny thing on the surface ("Satan disguises himself as an angel of light")
2. **Dark occult**: the underlying dark, occulted (hidden) reality

The Shiny Veneer

The "shiny veneer" describes the light occult. It's the deceptive shiny thing on the surface that tricks you into thinking the occult is harmless, benign, silly, useful, fascinating, interesting, spiritually evolutionary, sexy, and cool.

The devil will play off of what you desire. So, whenever you have a deep desire for power, knowledge, comfort, or healing, be careful, because the enemy could use that to trick you into the occult. I call these the "Big Four."

The shiny veneer of the occult is intensely tempting and equally deceptive, and it draws unsuspecting victims from any place on the planet. The occult is addictive and entrancing. It draws you into delusion and narcissism and it is extremely harmful to the soul.

The shiny veneer comes in the form of cultural acceptance of the occult. Nowadays occult items and beliefs are omnipresent in our consumer-driven culture, such that you might incorporate occultism into your life without batting an eye. Satan wants you locked into the shiny veneer so you'll lose yourself and won't be able to find your way out.

An Occult Worldview

Your worldview is the lens through which you perceive reality. Your worldview is the foundation upon which your values, beliefs, thoughts, and attitudes are built, and these fuel your emotions, actions, practices, and behaviors, which lead to the formation of habits and addictions.

An occult worldview is based on distortions about who you are as a person, who God is, and what your purpose is in the world. An occult worldview is self-centered and narcissistic, and it fuels the lie that you are equal to God.

This worldview is exactly what Satan wants for you, because it draws you away from God, keeps you out of the Kingdom, and leads to eternal death.

The core of this worldview is the attempt to seek salvation through your own actions and the achievement of self-serving goals. The core sin of this worldview is pride. The core theme of this worldview is idolatry.

An occult worldview is the deepest level of occult integration. You can get rid of addictions and habits and cut off occult practices, but underneath the practices are the thoughts and attitudes. Under those are the beliefs and values. And under those is the worldview.

What Stems from an Occult Worldview?

Your heart represents your innermost desires. What do you place on the throne of your heart? Upon what are you placing your affection and giving your attention? What do you focus on and worship? What you place on the throne of your heart develops into your worldview. The development of a worldview is about focus, attention, environment, exposure, and time.

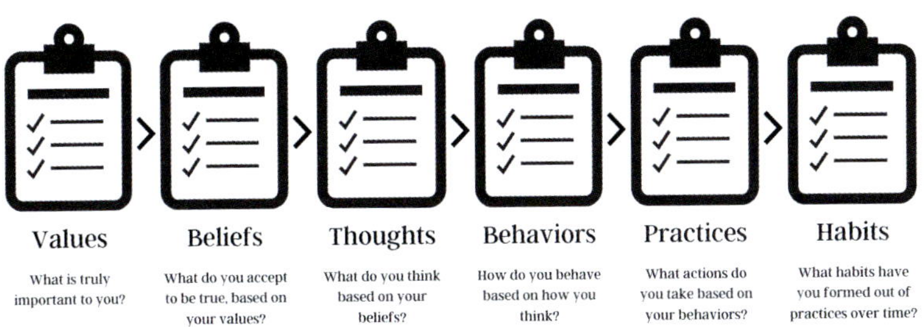

As you can see by this model, your worldview has a cascading effect on your life.

- Your worldview determines what you value.
- What you value determines what you believe.
- What you believe determines what you think.
- What you think determines how you behave.
- How you behave determines what you practice.
- What you practice determines your habits.

Characteristics of an Occult Worldview

An occult worldview can be characterized by the following:

- **Values**: knowledge and power gained through occult or other inadequate means
- **Beliefs**: distorted beliefs about God, humanity, and salvation, usually affirming gnosticism, reincarnation, universalism, channeling demons, invocation, and evocation
- **Thoughts**: narcissistic, destructive, prideful; practical ideation about invocation, and evocation of occult knowledge and/or power
- **Behavior**: self-serving inclinations and reactions that include impulses to interact with the occult
- **Practices**: engagement in occult practices
- **Habits**: habitual engagement in occult practices; obsession with and addiction to occult practices

Defining Invocation and Evocation

Occult practices involve two critical terms:

- **Invocation**: calling in
- **Evocation**: calling forth

While they manifest in different ways, all these practices are very enticing and deceptive in the world today. Our world has completely normalized these practices, and they are quite literally what opens the door to demonic contracts. Only by the Blood of Jesus Christ can these contracts be broken.

Through invocation and evocation, a person invites the demonic in and prepares to make contractual agreements with it. The demon offers something (such as power or knowledge), and the person accepts or receives what the demon has offered. The exchange point is the person's soul. As they give up more and more of their free will through choosing occult knowledge and power, they open themselves up to losing the capacities they still have control over.

Because the person is willing to give themselves up in worship to the demonic (whether they know what they are doing or not), this can result in demonic possession. In my case, I certainly did not understand that I was inviting or fraternizing with the demonic. But the reality is that that's exactly what I was doing. And, in my case, it did result in demonic possession.

Evocation, in modern occultism, is masked by words and phrases such as:

- "I call forth the elemental forces of the air, water, earth, fire."
- "I evoke the powers of universal spirit."
- "I summon the guardian spirits of protection."

Invocation, in modern occultism, is masked by some of the following words and phrases:

- "I call into me the powers of the universe for wisdom and guidance."
- "I invite source to fill me and heal me."
- "I am open and ready and willing to receive insights from the source of love and light."

My Story

Over time, the blend I was engaging in gave way to more of the occult and less of Christian practices. My worldview was shifting.

At a certain point, I ceased claiming to be a Christian and just accepted that I was something else entirely. It didn't happen overnight; it took a few years of allowing these practices to overtake my mind, body, and heart. Before I had my "gig is up" moment, I spent a full year in the occult without claiming any Christian identity. I was deluded into thinking everything was in alignment. Satan fueled my pride as I ate up the lies from the palm of his hand. Trigger warning: It got bad.

Channeling Demons

At a certain point, I started channeling demons. I had no idea they were demons until my "gig is up" moment (which I cover in the next chapter). Here is a summary of how it went down.

1. I started purchasing books on channeling. I was led toward these purchases by following satanic signs/wonders, otherwise known as synchronicities.
2. After learning about channeling, I attempted the practice of evocation. Within seconds, I summoned a demon into the room who pretended to be the Archangel Michael. This freaked me out — but not enough to stop me.
3. The very next day, I attempted scrying by filling a bathtub with water and entering an altered state of consciousness.[13] I evoked a demonic response immediately. A satanic sign/wonder appeared in the form of images and messages tracing across the surface of the water as clear as day, which I observed with my physical eyes.
4. I discovered subsequent synchronicities or confirmations about my experiences when I researched the images online. I found that the messages I channeled were, in fact, real concepts that existed. This opened up more occult concepts for me to research.
5. This landed me in occult media. I came in contact with channelers, and I started studying channeling heavily. I joined a cult of the conspiracy, ufology, New Age flavor.
6. I started doing seances and communicating openly with demons. They gave me "downloads," or dense packages of

[13] Scrying is a form of divination that involves entering an altered state of consciousness with the intention of focusing the mind on a reflective surface to ease the process of receiving occult wisdom.

information, that I would then go research. I found there were entire volumes of books written on the topics the demons were giving me. This included information on gnosticism, occult healing, reiki, Egyptian and Norse mythology, Sumerian history, extraterrestrial life, classified space programs, interdimensional travel, the quantum field, demonic communication, and spiritual evolution.

Ignoring God's Angels

God sent his angels to me more than once during my time in the occult, but there was a point during my deepest delusion year as an occultist when God sent his angels to me in a very pointed way. I was sitting on my bed doing a research project on miracles. This was the first time in a while that I had chosen a topic related to Christianity as opposed to the occult, and I started to delve into Marian research.

Suddenly, there were two angels standing in my room. They spoke to me, saying the tarot stuff needed to go. I was not supposed to be reading tarot, teaching tarot, developing frameworks around tarot, or engaging in tarot. They said it was a distraction.

There was a pause.

Then, one of the angels directly said, "*You are supposed to be working with Catholics.*"

I started to cry. The angels disappeared, although it seemed I could still feel the echo of their presence. I curled up in my bed and began processing this. Suddenly, I had an intense vision of my life that flashed before my eyes in a quick succession of images — all the moments leading up to that moment. I saw all the pain and trauma that had led me to choose to be so far away from God. I felt a warm embrace. I felt a call. As I cried, I felt a deep sense of yearning for God in my heart. I felt the distance between us. I felt the pain palpably, the pain I now know that God was beckoning me to give to Him that I might be healed.

Unfortunately, this event did not stop my pride. It did not cut off my desire to develop authority in occult circles. In fact, I decided to stop the research project on miracles altogether. I didn't know what to make of the angels. I certainly had no idea how to reconcile Christianity with my current path, or how any of this would sit with my group of occult friends and colleagues. The cult programming was deeply embedded into my psyche at this point.

I actually leaned in more heavily to my tarot projects and prepared for a conference where I would teach about my tarot archetype system. As an occultist, I was actually hardened to the good angels and what they were saying. My ears were deaf to their words. I continued to turn away through my actions, choosing the occult.

Demonic Possession: The Extraordinary Form of Satan

Demonic spirits seek to influence a person's thoughts, emotions, and behaviors, to distract and destroy, and to eventually lead the person's soul to eternal damnation. The deeper, more direct forms of demonic attack are commonly referred to in the Catholic Church as the "extraordinary form of Satan." These types of direct attacks are usually preceded by pacts and agreements the person makes with the demonic, engagement in the occult, or historical involvement by the person's family in the occult.

Disclaimer: Determining a person's spiritual status must be something left to professionals. It is not prudent to self-diagnose or assume that your circumstances are caused by demonic influence. If you believe you might have a spiritual issue, please contact your local diocesan office, and they will put you in touch with a priest who can assess your situation personally. The indicators listed here do not necessarily confirm demonic influence and should be analyzed in conjunction with a plethora of other psychological, physical, and psychospiritual considerations by licensed and authorized professionals.

- **Demonic oppression**: Intrusive, condemning, evil thoughts. This can appear in different forms, such as abnormal fear or paranoia, evil nightmares, or unexplained chronic depression.
- **Demonic obsession**: A more pointed form of oppression. The evil inspirations ramp up and actually seem targeted. The person will usually exhibit what appears to be an obsession with the occult, but this is really the person engaging in the inspiration of the demonic — it's actually the demonic obsession being manifested and observed through the person's behavior. At this point, there are most definitely pacts and agreements (secured either in the past or present) between the person and a demon or demons.
- **Demonic vexation**: A physical attack on the person, including scratches, bruises, marks, and other violent forms of physical attack.
- **Demonic possession**: Signs of possession include knowing the unknowable, an aversion to holy objects (holy water, sacraments), superhuman strength, speaking in other languages unknown to the afflicted, losing time or consciousness, not remembering things, and the inability to pray, receive the Eucharist, or enter a church.

Demonic Pacts and Agreements

Demonic agreements

A demonic agreement is a contract made with a demon through accepting an evil inspiration that gives Satan warrant to oppress the individual.

Demons cannot read your mind, but they can influence your thoughts. When you go along with a demonic inspiration (a lie), you then agree with what is false, giving the enemy license to oppress you.

Examples of demonic agreements:

- A demon delivers the inspiration that channeling is a way to access God. You agree and decide to amend your life and channel more often.
- A demon delivers the inspiration that you are more spiritually advanced than others because you practice manifestation. You agree and ruminate on the prideful thoughts this inspiration fueled.
- A demon delivers the inspiration that moon rituals are efficacious for attracting money. You research how to conduct a moon ritual because you believe this inspiration to be true.

Notice that each agreement results in the decision to amend your life toward the lie and away from Christ.

Advice: Taking on a regimen of mental prayer through the *Spiritual Exercises* of St. Ignatius helps to identify inspirations so you can get ahead of any temptation toward demonic agreements or pacts. Demonic inspirations should be rebuked in real time, and if already agreed to, severed and covered in the Blood of Jesus through prayer, repentance, and fasting.

Demonic pacts

A demonic pact is a contract made with a demon through an action inspired by the human will that gives Satan license to oppress the individual.

The degree to which the enemy has access to oppress is determined by many factors, including severity of sin, intensity of conscience, previous pacts, repetition, and environment. Remember, pacts are "signed" through an action taken by the human will.

Examples of demonic pacts:

- The practice of channeling (invocation and/or evocation)
- The practice of the law of attraction or manifestation (witchcraft)

- The practice of conducting occult rituals

Advice: Entering into a demonic pact is quite serious. You've leveraged your own human will to act upon a demonic influence in a way that demonstrates, through human action, an engagement with that inspiration. Pacts are harder to break than agreements because they require cutting off a practice, renouncing that practice, spending time examining the conscience, engaging in the sacraments of Reconciliation and the Eucharist, reforming one's worldview, undergoing therapy, and demonstrating — over time — the metanoia of the soul in severing this pact.

"I Just Dabbled"

When it comes to occult practices, you either did it, or you didn't do it; there is no middle ground. Please be warned, you don't only make a pact with a demon if you see a satanic sign and wonder and believe it. You can make a pact with a demon without even experiencing something that "works." *The pact is made through the act.*

You might think you are "safe" from any negative consequences of any past occult actions. You might say, "Well, I did witchcraft for ten years, but nothing ever worked, so I didn't really believe it. Nothing happened. So I really just dabbled." But then, when you seek to dismantle the occult strongholds, the demonic pacts become painfully obvious as you suddenly find yourself struggling against a surge of demonic vexation and obsession.

If there's anything close to a curse word to me that's not actually a curse word, it's the word *dabble*. Most people use this word to distance themselves from their sin, to attempt to diminish their culpability for engaging in occult practices, and to fuel their delusion that they didn't do anything all that bad. This is a tragic way of thinking that leaves you in a state of pride, refusing reconciliation in any form. It's only when you try to understand the depravity of your sin that you can start to be transformed. It is within the depths of metanoia that we are inspired to crawl to the Cross for salvation and forgiveness of our sins. Be warned: Pride doesn't work out well — for any of us.

What Is It Like to Be Demonically Possessed?

I experienced multiple instances of demonic possession during my time in the occult. I learned most of the occult practices and beliefs I engaged in while being part of a very large and popular cult of occultists who were into conspiracy media and ufology. Here is a summary of a few aspects of my own experience during that time that I think will bring clarity to the concept and provide deeper insight into what this can actually look like.

Keep in mind that some of these bullet points could also apply to someone who is not experiencing possession, but instead vexation or oppression. However, I include them so you can understand the things that were happening to me during the time I was going in and out of states of possession.

- Losing control of body faculties (demons forcing me to move when I didn't prompt myself to move)
- Feeling like a passenger in my own body
- Intense rage toward religious items that were in close physical proximity to me; throwing away religious items to decrease the torment
- Not knowing what was controlling my body or why I was doing something
- Repeated circumstances of demons (who I thought were good entities) telling me to get involved with a person (professionally or as a friend) and then seeing the relationship go south in tragic ways
- Feeling blessed by anything having to do with my career in the occult, while everything else in my life seemed cursed
- Surges of intense negative emotions that weren't my own
- Bouts of disorientation and dissociation from reality

- Knowing things I couldn't possibly know during seances and divination
- Randomly receiving dense packages of information related to the occult that I had never researched
- Speaking in demonic tongues during seances; not knowing what I was saying and being scared
- Viewing myself from out of my own body during seances
- Losing time

States of Possession

During tarot readings

Demons overtook my body when I did tarot readings for myself and others. When reading for others, I would step outside my body and fully dissociate. I was completely checked out. Sometimes I could hear a murmur of words and got the sense of a reading happening, and at the end of the reading, I would enter back into my body. At that moment, I usually would be greeted by the shocked face of the person sitting across from me. At times, they were visibly shaking and were stunned that I knew things they had never told anyone else. They were typically "glamoured" and had a certain excited electricity to them. They would exclaim how surprised they were that the tarot readings actually worked, and generally they were overjoyed at the empowering message I gave them and the clarity I provided.

I usually had no recollection of the content of the reading itself. I rationalized this phenomenon by claiming that tarot was my soul's "modality"; this was my gift — my soul talking to their soul. The reading was a purge, kind of like a confession for the person, so it didn't require my conscious mind to be present. We were communicating on a soul level with each other. Yikes.

One time, after I gave a man his first tarot reading, he said it resonated deeply, but also terrified him. He was so shocked at what I knew (things he had never told anyone) that he ran out of the room. I never spoke to him again.

Automatic writing

Sometimes demons would take over my body during channeling sessions. I would go into an altered state of consciousness, evoking and invoking the demonic. I would call out to "angels" or spiritual beings who would assist me by giving me esoteric knowledge. They would write through me.

At times I would actually lose time. I would "come to," so to speak, and look at pages and pages of writing that was highly specific — things about myself, my life, the larger story of the souls on this planet, our mission as a species, intricacies of occult power and knowledge, and how to perform certain rituals.

Overall, the enemy's tactic with automatic writing goes like this:

1. Tempt the human to invoke the demonic.
2. Once they invoke, enter into them.
3. Get them to write down things that will make them curious and lead them to think they are unique and have a special gift and call to bring this knowledge and information to the world.
4. Send signs and wonders so they will believe that the information holds significance.
5. Include enough information in the channeled writing to synchronize with other things that already exist on the Internet (because of so many people channeling demons and putting the information out there).
6. Watch the human get puffed up with hubris and become addicted to the "hit" the occult knowledge gives them.
7. Rinse and repeat.

9

THE GIG IS UP

1+ events destabilize occult worldviews. Take pause.

What Is a "Gig Is Up" Moment?

When you are functioning inside an occult worldview, suddenly, an event might occur that destabilizes that worldview. The "gig is up" moment happens when you suddenly begin to question the integrity of your worldview. This can come in many forms.

Here are some things you might start to question:

- the efficacy or validity of your practices and habits
- the integrity of your actions
- the truth of your beliefs and thoughts
- the value of what you hold to be important
- the validity of your view of God's character
- the reality of your perception

Sometimes the "gig is up" moment comes through the words of a friend, a well-placed phrase in a media production, or perhaps a Bible verse spoken to you while your heart is in a softened state. Either way, this moment rocks you. It makes you stop and wonder if you are on the right path.

God Pursues

I see this "gig is up" moment as a profound stirring of the Holy Spirit in your heart designed to awaken you out of the slumber of the occult.

Consider this: The Holy Spirit is working on a person throughout their whole life and then orchestrates this grand "gig is up" moment as a wake-up call, one preceding a call home! In many of the testimonies I hear, I can clearly see the Lord moving in the person's life at this time. And it's just so beautiful to see.

We cannot create or purposefully instigate the "gig is up" moment. It's a supernatural "God thing." You see, it's not easy to convince someone to drop their occult worldview. There has to be something significant, something radical, something loud that will jar them out of their stupor and rock their world. It has to be something that causes them to really stop and take a good, hard look at reality.

Although God is the author of the "gig is up" moment, He uses people to build up and lay the groundwork for these pivotal moments that can have a salvifically intense impact on the soul.

People often come to me with the desire to help wake someone up and get them out of the occult. There are strategies, yes. But the most important piece of advice I give is simply this: "Pray." God often provides whatever is needed to pull people away from the strong delusion of the occult. The "gig is up" moment manifests differently in every case. It's difficult to describe because it can come from a lot of places in a lot of ways. However it manifests, though, it creates a forceful wave that crests and breaks, leading to what appears to be an epiphany.

Merriam-Webster defines *epiphany* as "a usually sudden manifestation or perception of the essential nature or meaning of something; an intuitive grasp of reality through something (such as an event) usually simple and striking; an illuminating discovery, realization, or disclosure; a revealing scene or moment."[14]

Isn't it wonderful that the word *epiphany* also refers to the first manifestation of Christ to the Gentiles? In the case of someone in bondage to the occult, though, the "gig is up" moment is not a realization of Christ, but a destabilization of their occult worldview.

Worldview Destabilization

Just because an occultist has a "gig is up" moment, this does not mean they actually turn to Christ. Each of us has free will. We can choose where to turn. Some have a "gig is up" moment but never actually choose Christ.

Let's say you're an occultist who experiences a moment that makes you question your beliefs. If you have no Christian foundations, a long history of occultism, and are not surrounded by Christians, this can make the idea of choosing Christ as Lord more unlikely. But if you were raised Christian and have that foundation, it can occur to you more quickly to look to Christ to fill the Jesus-sized hole in your hearts.

Additionally, the nature of the circumstance surrounding the "gig is up" moment determines how effectively you turn to Christ. If the moment comes through a Christian channel, it might be easier. If you have no Christian foundation and discover a spiritual affliction that makes you question your practices, it can leave you stunned and confused if you don't have Christian help leading you to Christ. This can lead to a period of time that I've coined "the In-Between," which I cover in the next chapter.

[14] "Epiphany," *Merriam-Webster Dictionary*, https://www.merriam-webster.com/dictionary/epiphany.

My Story

It's hard for me to share my "gig is up" moment because the events surrounding it are deeply traumatic to relive and recount. I've left out certain things given the sensitive and dangerous nature of the situation. But I'll share what I can.

Picture my "gig is up" moment by visualizing these images:

- ✦ A mirror buckles under pressure and begins to fracture.
- ✦ A deck of cards shudders under the weight of gravity and begins to slip.
- ✦ A wave grows along the horizon and begins to crest.

The mirror shatters. The cards fall. The wave breaks.

My "gig is up" moment included the following buildup:

- ✦ I discovered that the leadership of the cult I was involved with was lying to people to obtain money, support, and adoration from their followers. When I confronted them, they threatened me and told me to stop asking questions.
- ✦ Occultists close to me claimed to be in contact with the same "higher-density beings" as me and told me we were both being influenced positively by the same beings. These occultists then betrayed me publicly in a really traumatic way. This immediately caused me to doubt the nature of these "higher-density beings."
- ✦ I constantly battled questions in my mind about why the industry would not approach or entertain the concept of evil on podcasts and radio shows when I would try to bring it up.
- ✦ I saw through the relativism of the spiritual beliefs I was engaging in. (I believed in objective truth.)
- ✦ I questioned if the beings with whom I was in contact were evil.
- ✦ I questioned if perceived extraterrestrial abductions were actually an indication of spiritual, physical, mental, and emotional abuse from evil spiritual entities.

- I wondered why I was being harassed and bullied by an entity the cult worshiped. My occult friends told me this was a positive spiritual being who was supposed to help humanity into the New Age of enlightenment.
- I heard voices in my head that weren't mine, and I couldn't get them out of my head. I can only describe this experience as feeling like mental rape.
- I had a spiritual entity attached to me that seemed nice at first and then proved to be cruel.
- I heard voices in my head telling me to do things I didn't want to do. If I didn't comply, they would attack me with severe panic and talk loudly in my head. This often led to me crying on the floor in a fetal position. Next, I experienced catatonic states and paranoia.
- I received warnings from many people about the dangerous nature of the cult I was involved in, and I encountered evidence of disturbing satanic practices.
- There were indicators that I was being groomed for nefarious purposes, the details of which I will not mention for consideration of my life and well-being. (A licensed professional specializing in cult snapping affirmed this analysis and encouraged this approach.)

My "gig is up" moment came through as a question in my head of just six words: *What if all this is demonic?*

The words hit me like a shock to my system. As soon as the realization occurred, the demons, now caught, turned on me.

The gig was up.

Immediately, it was as though Hell had broken loose in my room. Demons were laughing at me, jeering at me, intimidating me. I couldn't get their voices out of my head. It was as though someone had flipped a switch and many voices were suddenly screaming at the tops of their lungs.

The demons had concealed themselves from me by many masks to attempt to pull me into various conspiracist and ufological narratives. They presented as blue-gray aliens, large and small bird beings, Nordic-looking humans, and a plethora of other things. But they were now grotesque monsters, closing in on me from all sides.

For the first time in a long time, I ran and found a Bible. I curled up in the fetal position in my bed and prayed for God to show me something that would offer me a lifeline. I flipped the Bible open and began to read.

> Now concerning the coming of Our Lord Jesus Christ and our assembling to meet him, we beg you, brethren, not to be quickly shaken in mind or excited, either by spirit or by word, or by letter purporting to be from us, to the effect that the day of the Lord has come. Let no one deceive you in any way; for that day will not come, unless the rebellion comes first, and the man of lawlessness is revealed, the son of perdition, who opposes and exalts himself against every so-called god or object of worship, so that he takes his seat in the temple of God, proclaiming himself to be God. Do you not remember that when I was still with you I told you this? And you know what is restraining him now so that he may be revealed in his time. For the mystery of lawlessness is already at work; only he who now restrains it will do so until he is out of the way. And then the lawless one will be revealed, and the Lord Jesus will slay him with the breath of his mouth and destroy him by his appearing and his coming. *The coming of the lawless one by the activity of Satan will be with all power and with pretended signs and wonders, and with all wicked deception for those who are to perish, because they refused to love the truth and so be saved.* (2 Thess. 2:1–10, emphasis added)

Life-giving water flowed through the words into my mind and washed over my spirit. Scripture was coming alive. I flipped to another page.

> For the wrath of God is revealed from heaven against all ungodliness and wickedness of men who by their wickedness suppress the truth. For what can be known about God is plain to them, because God has shown it to them. Ever since the creation of the world his invisible nature, namely, his eternal power and deity, has been clearly perceived in the things that have been made. So they are without excuse; *for although they knew God they did not honor him as God or give thanks to him, but they became futile in their thinking and their senseless minds were darkened. Claiming to be wise, they became fools, and exchanged the glory of the immortal God for images resembling mortal man or birds or animals or reptiles.*
>
> Therefore God gave them up in the lusts of their hearts to impurity, to the dishonoring of their bodies among themselves, *because they exchanged the truth about God for a lie and worshiped and served the creature rather than the Creator, who is blessed for ever!* Amen. (Rom. 1:18–25)

This is all true! I exclaimed in my heart. I knew what I was reading was what I had been searching for all along. I'd heard these words (*how many times?*), but now they were coming alive with a deepened and more significant meaning that I hadn't had access to before.

I turned to one more passage.

> See to it that no one takes you captive by philosophy and empty deceit, according to human tradition, according to the elemental spirit of the world, and not according to Christ. For in him the whole fullness of deity dwells bodily, and you have been filled in him, who is the head of all rule and authority. (Col. 2:8–10)

The words hit me with a force I didn't anticipate. A gut-wrenching sob came from somewhere deep inside me. Suddenly, I was in outer space, standing at the very edge of reality. I became potently aware of my sin. I could feel in my body the reality of the choices I had made — every decision, every step away from God. It wasn't anything He did to walk away from me; I had walked away from Him. Now I was in outer darkness, drowning in my sin. The stain of sin was all over me, in my mind, on my body, in my heart, in my spirit. I felt cold. I was cast into the eternal darkness because of my own wretchedness.

Satan's Face, God's Grace

And then, I beheld Satan's face. There he was, looking me directly in the eyes.

He laughed.

I could see the joy in his eyes because I had fallen for his schemes. I had bought into the deception fully. Suddenly, I could feel the presence of the idols all around me. I could feel the heaviness, the weight of the stumbling blocks that were strewn between me and God. My eyes had been locked on the created, and I had forgotten about my cherished one, my own precious Creator. The depth of my sin toppled over me and threatened to crush me.

Satan sneered. Outer space became even colder and more desolate.

"God, save me!" I cried from the deepest recesses of my soul.

Within a millisecond, I felt the Lord swoop in and cover every single corner of my room. Satan was gone; the demons were gone; everything was still. God had answered my prayer. His warmth enveloped me.

I wept.

Part 2

Path to Freedom

THE IN-BETWEEN

Analyze belief systems. Seek solutions to reconcile beliefs.

COLOSSIANS ONE MOMENT

Turn away from the occult. Take action to choose Christ as Savior.

ENTER: THE WOODS

Spiritual attacks increase. Persevere. Build new worldview.

THE WORLD

Reenter society. Deeper surrender. Divine Mercy abounds.

THE CALLING

Hear and heed the call from the Lord to build up the Kingdom.

10

Consequences of Occult Engagement

If you break the first commandment and choose to directly contact satanic forces, your spiritual senses are darkened, damaged, and at times destroyed. Think of it this way: Your prayers are a line directly to God. When you engage in the occult, you sever that line. Of course, Jesus Christ has the power to reconcile all things, and just because a spiritual connection has been destroyed definitely doesn't mean that Jesus can't make all things new. He can and does! But it takes dedication and trust on the part of the victim.

In my experience, most people who are seeking to be free of the occult ask these three questions:

- How do I hear the voice of God?
- How do I pray?
- How do I know what is of God and what isn't?

Impact of the Occult upon the Spiritual Senses

If you are in occult bondage, this affects your spiritual senses, often incapacitating your ability to spiritually see, hear, and speak.

Eyes

As a victim of the occult, your spiritual eyes are blinded by pride, rendering you unable to see and recognize your sin and making it extremely difficult to repent and be reconciled to God.

The remedy to this is not easy, and most of the time requires some radical circumstance in your life to jolt you out of your spiritual blindness. It can be almost impossible to talk someone out of this state; instead, these wake-up calls are instigated by life situations that make one suspicious of one's own beliefs and practices.

A mature Christian at this point can come alongside you and lead you to Christ. (This is usually a matter of timing.)

Ears

As a victim in occult bondage, you lose the ability to hear God's voice; instead, you have directed your attention to demonic forces, received and integrated the information, and reinforced those lies through occult practices.

This makes it extremely difficult to discern the voice of God. The remedy for this is intentional immersion in the Word of God to break down strongholds, install the truth of Christ, and develop spiritual discernment.

Mouth

You no longer know how to speak to God because your mind, heart, and words have been continually given over to occult ideation and practices.

Plagued by distortions of the mind, you don't know the true character of God, and you often believe God to be nothing more than an impersonal, elemental force of nature. How can you talk to the personal God of all creation when you think He is a force of nature?

The remedy for this is spiritual formation, theological education, and learning how to pray.

The Fallacy of the Blend

Those held in occult bondage often think they can blend the occult with Christianity, and this blinds them to the reality that they are under the sway of an occult worldview. God's Word makes it clear, however, that light and darkness cannot coexist.

God is light, and in Him is no darkness at all.

> This is the message we have heard from him and proclaim to you, that God is light and in him is no darkness at all. If we say we have fellowship with him while we walk in darkness, we lie and do not live according to the truth; but if we walk in the light, as he is in the light, we have fellowship with one another, and the blood of Jesus his Son cleanses us from all sin. If we say we have no sin, we deceive ourselves, and the truth is not in us. If we confess our sins, he is faithful and just, and will forgive our sins and cleanse us from all unrighteousness. If we say we have not sinned, we make him a liar, and his word is not in us. (1 John 1:5–10)

The darkness does not even comprehend the light.

> The light shines in the darkness, and the darkness has not overcome it. (John 1:5)

Righteousness has no partnership with lawlessness.

> What partnership has righteousness with lawlessness? Or what fellowship has light with darkness? What accord has Christ with Belial? Or what portion does a believer share with an unbeliever? What agreement has the temple of God with idols? For we are the temple of the living God. (2 Cor. 6)

Approaching Deliverance

When it comes to approaching deliverance, it is imperative to drive home these two facts:

1. The occult is completely centered around self-absorption and pride.

2. Jesus is the exact opposite of pride. He humbled Himself, even to the point of offering up His entire self as a sacrifice for the sins of the whole world, that we might enter the Eternal Kingdom.

Pride and Jesus' humble sacrifice are in direct opposition to each other; they are antithetical. You cannot function inside the occult, harnessing satanic power and knowledge for your benefit on this planet, and expect to enter the Kingdom of God. You are in denial of your sin and your need for a savior.

If you have an occult worldview, you either ignore or deny the reality of sin and you reject the idea that Jesus is literally the only way into the Kingdom of God. There is no way you can be immersed in the works of Satan and also yield your heart to Jesus.

Shucking Off an Occult Worldview

Many who were engaged in the blend tell of a moment when they realized that their pride and blindness to the efficacy of Jesus' Blood kept them stuck in their sins. They were engaging in the occult as a shortcut to fulfill their worldly desires, and when they realized that Jesus is the only way to eternal life, they saw that the effects of their occult practices were, in truth, little more than dust. At some point they realized that it doesn't matter what Satan offers — it's all in an active state of perishing. And the great equalizer, death, reminds us that we can't take any of these things with us beyond this life. *Memento mori.*

The factors surrounding a soul in bondage waking up to the dire need and yearning to follow Christ differ from person to person, and casting off the occult worldview is an intense process. Depending on how totally the anchors have penetrated your soul, and how deeply the layers of distortion and sin have pulled you into delusion and hardheartedness, the reformation of your spiritual senses can take much time and intense dedication. These spiritual senses must be rebuilt through the giving of your life to Christ, followed by dedicated spiritual formation, an intentional prayer life, and consistent sacramental worship.

Four Factors of Deliverance

Deliverance is a hot-button topic with many nuances and different expressions depending on how you approach it. When it comes to providing answers about how deliverance works, it's important to provide a foundation so you understand the nuances the deliverance process harbors. The four factors of deliverance are:

1. Divine Providence and God's Sovereignty
2. Belief of the Afflicted
3. Repentance of the Afflicted
4. Prayers/Intercession of the Intercessor(s) and the Afflicted

Deliverance unfolds differently case by case. These four factors will help to provide a reference point if you're trying to figure out what's going on as you traverse an often disorienting process.

To develop this material, I present Scripture verses and references from the *Catechism of the Catholic Church* (CCC) that have been incredibly useful in my own experience with deliverance. I often give this material to people as they get started so that they have a baseline reference for the situation. Overall, when it comes to deliverance, these four factors are always at play.

Thank you, Lord Jesus, for delivering us from the dominion of darkness and transferring us into the Kingdom of Heaven!

11

Divine Providence and God's Sovereignty

Here are five key components of Divine Providence and God's sovereignty.

1. All things are created for God's glory.

God is a perfect and truly good God, who created all things for his glory and presents to humanity the free choice of reconciliation to Him through Jesus Christ, to be established as His people, to reside with Him in the New Heaven and New Earth.

> The glory of God consists in the realization of this manifestation and communication of his goodness, for which the world was created. God made us "to be his sons through Jesus Christ, according to the purpose of his will, to the praise of his glorious grace" (*CCC*, 294).

The nature of deliverance is for God to be glorified. "And call upon me in the day of trouble; I will deliver you, and you shall glorify me" (Ps. 50:15).

2. God's will shall be done.

Chapter 14 of the book of Wisdom describes the Providence of God, reflecting upon His faithfulness to carry humanity forward according to His divine plan, despite our weakness and frailty.

> One preparing for a voyage and about to traverse the wild waves cries out to wood more unsound than the boat that bears him, for the urge for profits devised this latter, and Wisdom the artisan produced it. But your providence, O Father! guides it, for you have furnished even in the sea a road, and through the waves, a steady path, showing that you can save from any danger, so that even one without skill may embark. (Wis. 14:1–4)

Divine Providence is God's action to bring about His divine purpose. Divine Providence is inevitable and cannot be thwarted. "So shall my word be that goes out from my mouth; it shall not return to me empty, but it shall accomplish that which I purpose, and prosper in the thing for which I sent it" (Isa. 55:11).

God has absolute sovereignty over all events. "Many are the plans in the mind of a man, but it is the purpose of the Lord that will be established" (Prov. 19:21).

3. Humans are given free will to choose God.

God understands our needs intimately, and we are told not to be anxious or worry about anything, but instead to seek the Kingdom of God. "Seek first his kingdom and his righteousness, and all these things shall be yours as well" (Matt. 6:33).

Creation was created by God as good, but also incomplete. The universe is in *statu viae*, which means it was created "in a state of journeying toward an ultimate perfection yet to be attained, to which God has destined it" (*CCC*, 302).

> He so orders all events within the universe, that the end for which it was created may be realized. That end is that all creatures should manifest the glory of God, and in particular, that man should glorify Him, recognizing in nature the work of His hand, serving Him in obedience and love, and thereby

attaining the full development of his nature and to eternal happiness in God.[15]

God does not force His Kingdom and partnership upon humanity. We are given the free will to choose to enter into a relationship with Him through accepting the salvation of our souls through Jesus Christ, and actively partnering with Him in the journey of theosis or sanctification.

4. Christians are called to accept God's sovereignty over suffering. Certain afflictions are not removed from us, not resulting from the judgment by God of our character, but that God might be glorified. Our sins, beliefs, and repentance are factors that play into liberation, but ultimately, God's will supersedes our actions. Our suffering does not necessarily mean we have sinned, lack belief, or lack repentance, but that God might be glorified. Jesus said about a man born blind, "It was not that this man sinned, or his parents, but that the works of God might be made manifest in him" (John 9:3).

Paul described his own affliction that he suffered willingly for whatever purpose the Lord had for it. "And to keep me from being too elated by the abundance of revelations, a thorn was given me in the flesh, a messenger of Satan, to harass me, to keep me from being too elated" (2 Cor. 12:7).

Conversely, God might allow suffering to bring us to full repentance. "The Lord is not slow about his promise as some count slowness, but is forbearing toward you, not wishing that any should perish, but that all should reach repentance" (2 Pet. 3:9).

We are in a grace period, the time of imperfection, the time in between Jesus conquering death and coming back to fully restore us to

15 "Providence," New Advent, https://www.newadvent.org/cathen/12510a.htm.

eternal life. In this time, we are given the option to choose life in Christ and so be perfected by the Holy Spirit working in us, for the fulfillment of God's plan and purpose for us. "For now we see in a mirror dimly, but then face to face. Now I know in part; then I shall understand fully, even as I have been fully understood" (1 Cor. 13:12).

Regardless of suffering being present in our lives, we know that God is sovereign over our situations. We are called to trust Him and know that we are divinely protected by the Blood of Jesus and are heirs to His eternal Kingdom.

We are called to work out our salvation every moment of our lives, to remain steadfast and vigilant, and to keep our eyes locked on Christ regardless of any suffering we endure. "Blessed is the man who endures trial, for when he has stood the test he will receive the crown of life which God has promised to those who love him" (James 1:12). We endure suffering willfully and with faith, knowing that in spite of our suffering, we are being perfected and brought to eternal redemption.

5. God has the authority to cast demons out of people.

Holy Scripture demonstrates that Jesus Christ has the authority to cast demons out of people.

> There was in their synagogue a man with an unclean spirit. And he cried out, "What have you to do with us, Jesus of Nazareth? Have you come to destroy us? I know who you are, the Holy One of God." But Jesus rebuked him, saying, "Be silent, and come out of him!" And the unclean spirit, convulsing him and crying with a loud voice, came out of him. (Mark 1:23–26)

The same anecdote is provided in Luke, which describes His authority and power to cast out demons. "And they were all amazed and said to one another, 'What is this word? For with authority and power he commands the unclean spirits, and they come out' " (Luke 4:36).

Components of Divine Providence and God's Sovereignty

1. God is perfectly good and kind and created all things for His glory.
2. God's will shall be done. His plans are irrefutable and inevitable.
3. God offers us the free will to accept salvation through Jesus Christ, which begins the process of theosis so we might enter the Kingdom of God for eternity. Although God is sovereign over all and His will shall be done, God does not force us to choose Him.
4. Despite the phenomenon of suffering, we as Christians are called to accept and rejoice in God's sovereignty and His Divine Providence over our sufferings, for His glorification and will to be done through us in any way. God is faithful to His children.
5. God has the sovereign authority and power to cast out demons.

12

Belief of the Afflicted

Our beliefs play a critical role in deliverance from demonic oppression. There are three key concepts about belief for the afflicted to understand. First, the Bible provides accounts of deliverance based on the faith of the afflicted. Second, the gospel awakens faith. Third, expression of true faith takes dedication and persistence. We will go deep into these three concepts in this chapter.

Three Key Beliefs

1. Blind men were healed because of their belief.

> And as Jesus passed on from there, two blind men followed him, crying aloud, "Have mercy on us, Son of David." When he entered the house, the blind men came to him; and Jesus said to them, "Do you believe that I am able to do this?" They said to him, "Yes, Lord." Then he touched their eyes, saying, "According to your faith be it done to you." And their eyes were opened. (Matt. 9:27–30)

The word *faith* in this passage is the Greek word *pistis,* meaning "gift from God," and is "never something that can be produced by people … for the believer is 'God's divine persuasion' — and therefore distinct from human belief (confidence), yet involving it. The Lord continuously births faith in the yielded believer so they can know what He prefers, i.e. the persuasion of His will."[16] The core of this passage refers to the receptivity of the believer. *Pistis* means "It is God's warranty that guarantees the fulfillment of the revelation He births within the receptive believer."[17]

2. Faith is awakened by the message of salvation in Christ.

Faith is awakened by hearing the truth of the gospel — that is, our salvation in Christ.

- "So faith comes by hearing [what is told], and what is heard comes by the preaching [of the message that came from the lips] of Christ (the Messiah Himself)." (Romans 10:17, AMP)
- "Consequently, faith comes from hearing the message, and the message is heard through the word about Christ." (Romans 10:17, NIV)

Before Jesus cast out the demon possessing the boy in Mark 9, there was an interesting exchange between the father and Jesus. The father said, " 'If you can do anything, have pity on us and help us.' And Jesus said to him, 'If you can! All things are possible to him who believes.' Immediately the father of the child cried out and said, 'I believe; help my unbelief!' " (Mark 29:22–24). Jesus then rebuked the demon and it came out of the boy.

"I believe, help my unbelief!" The word *believe* in this passage is the Greek word *pisteuó*, meaning:

- conviction and trust to which a man is impelled by a certain inner and higher prerogative and law of his soul
- absolutely to trust in Jesus or in God as able to aid either in obtaining or in doing something

[16] "Pistis," *Strong's Greek Concordance*, https://biblehub.com/greek/4102.htm.

[17] Ibid.

- persuading oneself (human believing) and with the sacred significance of being persuaded by the Lord (faith-believing).[18]

The father says, "Help my unbelief," or *apistia,* meaning "unfaithfulness, distrust, want of faith, or no-faithfulness."[19]

The request the father made to Jesus here, the cry for help, or *boétheó,* is the active word and really the most interesting part of this passage. In the original language, *boétheó* was originally a military word, responding to a critical, urgent need; in Homer's poetry, it is used to signify a *war cry. Boé* means an "intense exclamation" and *theō* means "run; to run and meet an urgent distress call (cry for help); to deliver help, and quickly respond to an urgent need (intense distress)."[20]

Jesus is the one who answers our cry for salvation. We must cry out in urgent need of salvation so Jesus will respond and deliver us. It is the human awareness of sin and the cry for salvation through Jesus that results in the faith given to us by God.

3. An expression of true faith often takes dedication and persistence. Our faith is a critical component of deliverance, because God does not force a relationship on us; he gives us free will to believe in him.

"Behold, I stand at the door and knock; if any one hears my voice and opens the door, I will come in to him and eat with him, and he with me" (Rev. 3:20). This passage describes a person who hears God's voice, makes moves to receive the message of salvation (opens the

[18] "Pisteuó," *Strong's Greek Concordance,* https://biblehub.com/greek/4100.htm.

[19] "Apistos," *Strong's Greek Concordance,* https://biblehub.com/greek/570.htm.

[20] "Boétheó," *Strong's Greek Concordance,* https://biblehub.com/greek/997.htm.

door), and then experiences the exchange of being received and reconciled to Christ.

We are called to be persistent and endure, to continually seek the Lord. It is not a one-time choice, but the willful choice of a lifetime, a choice made over and over with every moment and fiber of our being. "For you have need of endurance, so that you may do the will of God and receive what is promised" (Heb. 10:36). "He who endures to the end will be saved" (Matt. 24:13).

"Submit yourselves therefore to God. Resist the devil and he will flee from you" (James 4:7). This passage has been improperly brandished to mean that anyone who claims to be a Christian cannot be oppressed by the devil. This is absolutely not true, and this nonchalant perspective is exactly the approach the devil wants us to take.

This perspective also completely misses the core message of this passage, which actually seeks to present a potent lesson about resistance. The Greek word for *resist* in this passage, *anthistémi*, means the following:

- take a complete stand against; a 180-degree, contrary position
- establish one's position publicly by conspicuously "holding one's ground"
- refuse to be moved ("pushed back")
- oppose fully, forcefully declare one's personal conviction (where one unswervingly stands)
- keep one's possession; ardently withstand, without giving up (letting go)

Anthistémi is a military term in classical Greek (used by Thucydides and others) meaning "to strongly resist an opponent" or to "take a firm stand against."

This word indicates a resoluteness and firmness of mind and heart, a confident intention to fix our eyes upon Christ and to turn our backs toward evil. When it comes to deliverance, faith in Christ and the desire to resist, or *anthistémi,* can take time depending on our hearts and minds, and these often require dedicated spiritual formation to evoke metanoia.

Furthermore, Ephesians 6 reminds us to "stand firmly" against the strategies and deceits of the devil, for we are not wrestling against flesh and blood but against the spiritual forces of wickedness in the heavenly spheres. This is why we are called to affirm our salvation in Christ and remain tethered to the Word of God at all times, which assists us in the raging spiritual battle.

Components of Belief of the Afflicted

1. Holy Scripture references Jesus healing and delivering based on the faith of the afflicted.
2. Faith is awakened by the afflicted hearing the gospel of Christ.
3. An expression of true faith takes dedication and persistence.

13

Repentance of the Afflicted

Repentance and faith often precede deliverance. If we do not have faith or repentance, why would the Lord deliver us? The Lord is sovereign and therefore can do whatever He wills.

However, taking into consideration all factors of deliverance, the Lord will wait for a person to come to faith and repentance before deliverance will occur. Moreover, faith and repentance of the afflicted are just factors in deliverance, not the whole picture.

This means it could be the Lord's will to not deliver us from some forms of affliction (see the example of Paul and the demon that the Lord allowed to afflict him to prevent hubris in 2 Corinthians 12:7).

That said, we also know that the Lord is reliable and faithful to His word, and it is through the Blood of Christ that we are delivered into the Kingdom of God.

Repentance and faith often precede a deeper acceptance of forgiveness from God, which commonly blossoms out of the person into an urge to forgive others. When an afflicted person suddenly feels the draw to forgive others related to traumas from the past, this usually marks the beginning of much-needed healing. Forgiveness opens a person up to deeper levels of deliverance from evil and draws them into closer communion with the Lord.

Four Key Truths

1. The Blood of Christ is the doorway into the Kingdom of God.
We enter the Kingdom of God through the Blood of Jesus Christ. And after entering through that doorway, we are confidently able to hold fast without wavering in our hope for eternal salvation.

> Therefore, brethren, since we have confidence to enter the sanctuary by the blood of Jesus, by the new and living way which he opened for us through the curtain, that is, through his flesh, and since we have a great priest over the house of God, let us draw near with a true heart in full assurance of faith, with our hearts sprinkled clean from an evil conscience and our bodies washed with pure water. Let us hold fast the confession of our hope without wavering, for he who promised is faithful. (Heb. 10:19–23)

That said, we are also called to remain vigilant and stay to the end to be saved. This requires that we hold fast to our confession and continue to grow in holiness as we are made perfect by the power of the Holy Spirit working in us.

2. The afflicted must continually repent with a penitent heart to rid themselves of Satan's influence.

> If my people who are called by my name humble themselves, and pray and seek my face, and turn from their wicked ways, then I will hear from heaven, and will forgive their sin and heal their land. (2 Chron. 7:14)

We know that God has made promises to His children. But the question becomes, how do we know if we actually are His children? There are steps to take to fully lean into Christ that bring us under His lordship and protection. Once those steps are taken and faith is clearly demonstrated, it is more likely that the Lord would allow a spiritual affliction to be alleviated.

Conversely, the Lord might deliver us to bring us to an even deeper level of faith and repentance, due to the working of the Holy Spirit in us. Usually, this is a process that involves a combination of both concepts: one step forward of repentance, another step forward of deliverance, and so forth. Deliverance occurs over time and with dedication, continued and deepening levels of repentance, and growing faith.

3. Confession can assist the afflicted with repentance and deliverance.
"If we confess our sins, he is faithful and just, and will forgive our sins and cleanse us from all unrighteousness" (1 John 1:9). Purification and sanctification are processes that take a lifetime of dedication and commitment. Through Holy Scripture, the Holy Spirit comes into us and changes us, renews our minds, and brings us to repentance. As we hear the Word and integrate its truth into our lives, we experience greater freedom from bondage. Receiving forgiveness from God through confession orients a person's heart toward the forgiveness of others.

4. The afflicted must have faith, renounce the enemy, repent, forgive and receive forgiveness, and demonstrate amendment of life to maximize deliverance results.
The process begins with faith, and then moves into renunciation, repentance, and demonstrated amendment of life.

- "He who conceals his transgressions will not prosper, but he who confesses and forsakes them will obtain mercy" (Prov. 28:13).
- "Bear fruit that befits repentance" (Matt. 3:8).
- "The Lord is not slow about his promise as some count slowness, but is forbearing toward you, not wishing that any should perish, but that all should reach repentance" (2 Pet. 3:9).

- "Those whom I love, I reprove and chasten; so be zealous and repent" (Rev. 3:19).
- "Draw near to God and he will draw near to you. Cleanse your hands, you sinners, and purify your hearts, you men of double mind" (James 4:8).
- "For I have no pleasure in the death of any one, says the Lord God; so turn, and live" (Ezek. 18:32)

Components of Repentance of the Afflicted

1. The Blood of Jesus Christ is the doorway into the Kingdom of God. This truth must first be integrated into the person's heart in order for repentance to occur.
2. The afflicted must continually repent with a penitent heart so as to rid themselves of Satan's influence.
3. Confession can assist the afflicted with repentance.
4. The afflicted must have faith, renounce the enemy, repent, forgive and receive forgiveness, and demonstrate amendment of life to maximize deliverance results.

14

Prayers of the Intercessor and Afflicted

Inviting a community of your fellow Christians to pray for you as you are getting free and anchoring your heart to Christ is advisable. The path of deliverance is isolating enough, and letting people you trust into the process can help you feel less alone. God calls us into community. Finding a community of Christians whom you trust to pray with you can teach you about prayer, strengthen you when disoriented, and help you persevere in your path as a believer.

The Importance of Prayer

1. Christians are called to pray unceasingly to effectively stand against the devil's schemes.

"Be sober, be watchful. Your adversary the devil prowls around like a roaring lion, seeking some one to devour" (1 Pet. 5:8).

The call here is to pray. The word *sober-minded* is the Greek word *nēpsate,* which means "be of sound judgment and sober [spirit] for the purpose of prayer."[21]

2. Some demonic attachments can only be removed through prayer.

Holy Scripture describes the disciples not being able to cast out a demon, and Jesus explained that there are nuances to the efficacy of them

[21] "Népsate," *Strong's Greek Concordance,* https://biblehub.com/greek/ne_psate_3525.htm.

casting out the demonic. Whereas the demons are entirely subject to the authority of Jesus Christ, the disciples do not share the same level of efficacy in casting them out.

> But Jesus took him by the hand and lifted him up, and he arose. And when he had entered the house, his disciples asked him privately, "Why could we not cast it out?" And he said to them, "This kind cannot be driven out by anything but prayer and fasting." (Mark 9:27–29)

"Why could we not cast it out?" The Greek word for *cast* here is *ekballo*, which means "to throw, cast, put out, banish, bring forth, produce."[22]

Jesus answered that this kind cannot "come out" except by *proseuché*, or "prayer to God."[23]

Jesus clearly calls us to pray for deliverance, and so learning how to pray and establishing a dedicated prayer life are central aspects of getting free and learning how to walk in your identity in Christ.

3. The faith of the intercessor is a factor in the efficacy of deliverance.

> And when they came to the crowd, a man came up to him and kneeling before him said, "Lord, have mercy on my son, for he is an epileptic and he suffers terribly; for often he falls into the fire, and often into the water. And I brought him to your disciples, and they could not heal him." And Jesus answered, "O faithless and perverse generation, how long am I to be with you? How long am I to bear with you? Bring him here to me." And Jesus rebuked him, and the demon came out of him, and the boy was cured instantly. Then the disciples came to Jesus

[22] "Ekballo," *Strong's Greek Concordance*, https://biblehub.com/greek/1544.htm.

[23] "Proseuché," *Strong's Greek Concordance*, https://biblehub.com/greek/4335.htm.

> privately and said, "Why could we not cast it out?" He said to them, "Because of your little faith. For truly, I say to you, if you have faith as a grain of mustard seed, you will say to this mountain, 'Move from hence to yonder place,' and it will move; and nothing will be impossible to you." (Matt. 17:14–20)

> Therefore confess your sins to one another, and pray for one another, that you may be healed. The prayer of a righteous man has great power in its effects. (James 5:16)

The Body of Christ is called to intercede on behalf of the spiritually afflicted. The Lord listens to the prayers of the faithful. Faithful intercession helps to bring souls from bondage into faith, repentance, and full conversion. The Lord calls both the afflicted and intercessors to pray for the deliverance of souls.

The Holy Spirit empowers the Body of Christ through gifts of faith, discernment, and intercession to bring the afflicted to liberation.

4. The afflicted must prayerfully endure and remain faithful through trials. They must take up their cross and follow Jesus.

As an afflicted person goes through the process of truly repenting and coming to faith, he might suffer during a period of spiritual affliction. This is a time of reflection upon past sins and usually is experienced in conjunction with not having fully given one's heart to Christ.

This is a middle-ground area where you are engaged in a spiritual struggle between the light and darkness. You must remain faithful during this time. This time tempers you, and you will learn many things about entering into a true relationship with the Lord and growing in faithfulness if you stand firm during this time.

The main biblical concepts that you should cling to during this period include passages about God's promises to His people, God's protection of His children, and the inheritance He gives to those who have faith in Christ. Focusing on these three key aspects of God's plan will help tether you to the truth of Christ as you go through the deliverance process.

- "No temptation has overtaken you that is not common to man. God is faithful, and he will not let you be tempted beyond your strength, but with the temptation will also provide the way of escape, that you may be able to endure it" (1 Cor. 10:13).
- "And he called to him the multitude with his disciples, and said to them, 'If any man would come after me, let him deny himself and take up his cross and follow me' " (Mark 8:34).
- "Seek the LORD while he may be found; call on him while he is near. Let the wicked forsake their ways and the unrighteous their thoughts. Let them turn to the LORD, and he will have mercy on them, and to our God, for he will freely pardon" (Isa. 55:6–7).

5. Deliverance prayers are one aspect of a larger deliverance process. One question that often arises is: Why would the Lord not deliver someone from spiritual affliction? Let's look at Matthew 12.

> "When the unclean spirit has gone out of a man, he passes through waterless places seeking rest, but he finds none. Then he says, 'I will return to my house from which I came.' And when he comes he finds it empty, swept, and put in order. Then he goes and brings with him seven other spirits more evil than himself, and they enter and dwell there; and the last state of that man becomes worse than the first. So shall it be also with this evil generation." (Matt. 12:43–45)

Given that you can put yourself in a much worse condition if you get free of the demonic and then turn back to your old ways, I believe we must consider the concept of God's mercy in this case.

Let's say a person is not fully repentant, or perhaps they don't fully believe in Jesus Christ. If the Lord allowed them to be freed of the demonic influence, they would end up in a worse state than before. Does the Lord prevent deliverance in some cases to prevent the worsening of a spiritual issue?

Jesus Christ casts out demons in Holy Scripture with no issue whatsoever. However, Holy Scripture also makes it clear that the apostles and disciples do not share the same level of success. Jesus Christ is God; therefore, the demons obey Him. However, Jesus explains that the apostles' lack of faith and prayer prevented them from expelling the demonic.

Additionally, a warning is given that if someone is freed of the demonic without filling their hearts with the Holy Spirit, they will find themselves in a much worse situation. Taking a holistic view of deliverance, it's important to consider all factors and diligently work to bring the afflicted to faith, with repentance, through renunciation, toward full amendment of life.

Components of Prayers of the Intercessor and Afflicted

1. Christians are called to pray unceasingly to effectively stand against the devil's schemes.
2. Some demonic attachments can only be removed through prayer.
3. The faith of the intercessor is a factor in the efficacy of deliverance.
4. The afflicted must prayerfully endure and remain faithful through trial. They must take up their cross and follow Jesus.
5. Deliverance prayers are one aspect of a larger deliverance process.

15

THE IN-BETWEEN

Analyze belief systems. Seek solutions to reconcile beliefs.

In this chapter, I will attempt to capture what it can be like for you in between the time you experience your "gig is up" moment and before you surrender to Christ as savior, what I call the "Colossians One Moment."

> He has delivered us from the dominion of darkness and transferred us to the kingdom of his beloved Son, in whom we have redemption, the forgiveness of sins. (Col. 1:13–14)

Sometimes the Colossians One Moment happens immediately following the "gig is up" moment. Sometimes it will actually require multiple "gig is up" moments before someone turns to Christ. There are many factors at play that influence the timing here, including:

- the nature of the "gig is up" moment
- the environment surrounding you
- the level of access you have to a Christian support system
- the status of your heart

To capture turning to Jesus in one passage, it looks like this:

> A new heart I will give you, and a new spirit I will put within you; and I will take out of your flesh the heart of stone and give you a heart of flesh. (Ezek. 36:26)

The In-Between is the time when you know there's something wrong with the occult but haven't yet embarked on:

- the ontological moment of change that occurs in a person who becomes a new creation through Christ (if you're a brand-new Christian)
- the surrender to that ontological change (if you're a baptized Christian)

"If any one is in Christ, he is a new creation; the old has passed away, behold, the new has come" (2 Cor. 5:17). This change happens at Baptism, but then there must also be a continual choice to honor that sacrament and to lean into your faith, walk with Jesus, and stay the course. The Colossians One Moment happens when you surrender and lean in.

In my case, I was baptized as a baby. I was close to the Lord until college and then strayed and wandered. I got lost, but Jesus came after me and called me home. I needed to go through a reversion to come back under the headship of Christ, be cleansed from my sins, and be brought out of mortal sin and back into a state of grace. My darkened understanding had pulled me toward sin, and I had lived in sin for years. After the gig was up, I went through an in-between period before submitting fully to Christ's authority.

During this in-between time, I immersed myself in the Word, allowing the Holy Spirit to work on my heart, softening me and bringing light to my senses until I could receive God's grace and mercy and come back to my senses in Christ. I finally submitted fully when I decided to follow Him completely. I actually moved across the country for a period of time to immerse myself in reforming my beliefs and practices.

Think about the In-Between as the time it takes for you to realize that Jesus has left the ninety-nine sheep to search for and find the one lost lamb (see Luke 15:4–7). That "one" is you.

Cultural Traps in the In-Between

Because of the world we live in, we can get trapped in the In-Between and never actually choose Christ.

After interviewing people from around the world who were at various stages on the deliverance roadmap, I discovered some major cultural traps that can distort a person's worldview and hold them in bondage:

- **Gnosticism**: a draw to "go within" for answers
- **Eastern practices**: theological confusion
- **Human Potential Movement (HPM)**: the view that we can heal ourselves with our own minds
- **Unconventional health**: the many occult practices based upon alternative healing methods that conflate spiritual healing with physical healing
- **Law of Attraction**: a faulty belief that we can attract what we desire through the power of positive thinking
- **Drug culture**: a fog of confusion that negatively impacts decision-making abilities
- **Entertainment cults**: cult worldviews that lead to idolatry
- **Modern occultism**: pacts and agreements with the demonic
- **Deconstructionism**: theological distortions and rebellion
- **Destructive feminism**: radical feminist worldviews
- **Conspiracist worldviews**: paranoia and distrust

My Story

I wrote a song immediately after my "gig is up" moment and right before I fled the state to seek sanctuary with a group of Christians. Written a few days before I traveled across the country in fear of my life from angry occultists with a vendetta against me, it captures my heart in the In-Between state.

As you read the lyrics, you can feel my inner turmoil, my lament toward the people who sought to take me out, my crying out for the state of their souls, my confusion for the state of my own soul. You can also see glimpses of how my heart's softened state was in a prime condition for Jesus to enter into my life to begin healing me and delivering me from bondage.

"The In-Between"

Not too much in the middle when you're in the In-Between
When you spent your time running in circles
Spent your time saying things that you don't really mean
Not too much to the riddle when you're in the In-Between
'Cause you're too busy running from questions
When the answer's in your face like an empty guillotine
Fortress built upon lies
A mirage of paradise
Lost to a spirit of delusion
Comforted and hypnotized
Realize the disguise
Before the stronghold is eternalized
And when the mist of the veil is lifted
Way up high above the trees
You can try to fly away but the spell is broken
Cast your little circle from your quote-unquote enemies
Running from the devil, but he's in your mind

And you can't deny the blame when your hands ain't tied
When the blood from your fingers makes the reaper's eyes wide
Will he come for you when the storm is rising?
Capsize. Will you capsize?
Walk the plank or paralyze?
Will you find the other side?
Exchange your heart and catalyze?
Into the depths to baptize
Release the bonds and see the light
Metamorphosis into genesis

Burning Bridges

After I cried out for God to save me, He immediately started showing me what to do. I left the cult. I threw away thousands of dollars' worth of occult items. I burned my tarot business to the ground and refunded all payments for upcoming readings. After weeks of depression, tears, and demonic vexation, I went live on my YouTube channel and apologized to my followers, explaining that I had been terribly deceived and that occult practices were severely dangerous to the soul. I started reading the Bible on the live stream, but the stream started cutting out. I received multiple e-mails after the fact from people saying that when I started to read, they got a horrible headache and had to turn the stream off. People also reported the audio getting scratchy as soon as I began warning against tarot and returned to normal as soon as I moved to a different topic. When I finished the live stream, I knew it was time to leave the Internet.

The cult declared me a detractor and launched a character assassination campaign against me. And that was the minor part. I, along with others, experienced stalking and threats to the point where the FBI got involved. I was in physical danger, and others around me were too. I cut off all communication with everyone — I'm not exaggerating when I say we feared for our lives. I became a literal recluse.

We Wrestle Not . . .

> Finally, be strong in the Lord and in the strength of his might. Put on the whole armor of God, that you may be able to stand against the wiles of the devil. For we are not contending against flesh and blood, but against the principalities, against the powers, against the world rulers of this present darkness, against the spiritual hosts of wickedness in the heavenly places. Therefore take the whole armor of God, that you may be able to withstand in the evil day, and having done all, to stand. (Eph. 6:10–13)

This became my anthem. I saw on the spiritual level what was going on, and I did not land blame or rage on those who persecuted me. I forgave them because they knew not what they did. They couldn't see. The rumor in the cult was that I had lost my mind by becoming a Christian. The cult leader publicly called it "end-times madness." The followers spread the rumor that I had become a nun and joined a convent. All this was occurring at the same time as the threats, the stalking, and the federal officials getting involved. It was scary.

I knew God's angels were fighting battles in the heavenly spheres. God had me covered. I was hiding in Him. The earthly threats were only temporary and could not last forever. Even when things got really scary on that front, I knew that these people had surrendered to the demons that controlled them. They were blind and deaf and operating within a completely darkened worldview.

I prayed for their souls. I remembered constantly my own deliverance, and I thanked the Lord for saving my life, pulling me out of bondage, and opening my eyes. I remembered as often as I could that "we wrestle not."

Demonic Vexation

The demons were having a party around me as they bullied me deeper into isolation and desolation. At night I would lie in the fetal position, hold my Bible, and shake. After finally crying myself to sleep, I would have nightmares of being dragged down into Hell. The demons would reach up through my bed and grab at my back while angels fought overhead. I knew there was a battle over my soul going on.

I remember hearing a voice repeatedly tell me, "God is fighting your battles. Stand firm." I knew it was true with every fiber of my being. I didn't move.

After one particularly horrific night of demons attempting to drag me through the bed with their long, claw-like fingers, I went into the bathroom to wash my face. I looked in the mirror and felt pain in my back. I turned around and lifted up my shirt. There were bruise marks on my back in the shape of fingerprints. It was at this moment that I knew I was in over my head.

"You need to go to the Catholic Church. Go to the Bible. Look at the evil. Look at the exorcisms," I heard the Lord say. This was the same directive He had given me years earlier. I needed help.

I went to my childhood church, attended Mass, and then waited to speak with the priest afterward. He was chatting with some other women. It appeared they were close friends. He looked at me and then looked away a few times. It was clear I was the only one in line and that I was waiting to talk to him. He continued to ignore me. I went back three weeks in a row and the same thing happened each time.

I felt like I was cursed. I didn't know what to do. Was it my fault? Did I have some kind of barrier around me keeping me from help? I prayed for God to show me what He wanted me to do. Even my previous church friends wanted nothing to do with me. I was an outcast.

Four Gateway Factors

Going back to the gateway factors from the very beginning of the deliverance roadmap, we must consider something here. When it comes to the In-Between, the gateway factors play a part in the path toward the Colossians One Moment, but now we are going to shift the perspective and look at them from a slightly different angle.

Whereas there were factors that drew me into the occult, there were also factors that played into my eventual turning toward Christ:

- **Family history**: Since my family was devoutly Christian, I was quickly drawn back to reading the Bible and going to church immediately following my "gig is up" moment. I had a support system there to encourage me in these practices.
- **Childhood**: Because of my upbringing in the Faith, I was raised with a firm Christian foundation. I was in a worship band growing up and I played worship music as an adult, so turning to worship songs for healing and time with the Lord happened quickly after my Colossians One Moment.
- **Bridge to Christ**: After everything blew up in my face and I realized I had been deceived, the Bible and prayer were the first things I turned to.
- **Character assessment**: I found myself in a state of humiliation and embarrassment over my sin, devastation at the thought of misleading thousands of people into falsehood, and despair over actions that truly grieved the Lord. I hadn't considered or accepted that reality before.

Due to the state of my heart in the In-Between, I was primed to take action toward Christ sooner rather than later. A key person who helped to draw me back to Christ was my mother. She was by my side the whole time, sharing Scripture with me even when I was lost. She continually prayed with me and for me, set a good Catholic example, and extended the love of Christ to me every step of the way.

Timing and Circumstances

The time between a "gig is up" moment and coming to Christ plays out in different ways for every person leaving the occult. Your upbringing and surroundings largely determine if you will have an immediate inclination to turn toward Christ after rejecting the occult. Sometimes it takes a bit more time for other circumstances to fall into place for you to see turning to Christ as a viable option.

16

COLOSSIANS ONE MOMENT

Turn away from the occult. Take action to choose Christ as Savior.

Taking Action

A Colossians One Moment requires that you take action toward Christ. It's not enough to throw away occult items. It's not enough to halt an occult practice. Turning away from something is one thing. But turning toward Christ is something different entirely

So the question becomes, "How do you take action toward choosing Christ?"

This is a critical question for everyone, but especially when you're coming out of the occult. Often people have a lot of false beliefs about the world and Christianity as a whole and what it even means to follow Jesus. I always recommend starting with the Nicene Creed.

Studying the Nicene Creed

In order to be a professed Christian, you must first know what it means to be a Christian. So I always recommend that a person who wants to understand what they are signing up for start with learning about the Nicene Creed.[24]

Reading it is a start, but when working with an afflicted person, I have them analyze it line by line. They read a line and then find Scripture references that affirm it. Next they reflect on it and study how that aspect of the Creed contradicts the occult. They list whichever occult beliefs or practices do not align with that aspect of the Creed. Seeing these concepts side by side really helps them to discover just how different the occult is from Christianity.

After this exercise, the person knows exactly what the Christian faith professes and how it is in direct opposition to occult beliefs and practices. This gives the person the tools to understand the difference between occult worldviews and the Christian worldview, whether they choose to give their lives to Christ or not.

Some of the major aspects of the Nicene Creed that stand against the occult are as follows:

- I believe in one God.
- I believe in one Lord Jesus Christ, the only begotten Son of God.
- For us men and for our salvation He came down from Heaven.
- He was incarnate of the Virgin Mary.
- He will come again in glory to judge the living and the dead.
- I believe in the Holy Spirit . . . who proceeds from the Father and the Son.

[24] "Beliefs and Teachings: What We Believe," United States Conference of Catholic Bishops, https://www.usccb.org/beliefs-and-teachings/what-we-believe.

- I believe in one, holy, catholic, and apostolic Church.
- I confess one Baptism for the forgiveness of sins.

I've seen ex-occultists have some really incredible epiphanies when conducting this exercise. Here are a few of my favorites:

We believe in one Lord, Jesus Christ . . . through Him all things were made. *"New Agers believe Jesus is just a good teacher, and this shows that He is the Lord, through whom all things were made."*

We believe in one God . . . of all that is seen and unseen. *"This dispels the New Age lies of Divinity of Man, God is impersonal, pantheism, Monism, nature worship, and panentheism. According to Scripture, there is only one God. He created all. Though He is over all and through all (see Ephesians 4:6), as our great maker, He is also separate from His creation. He is the Almighty, the Creator, the Alpha and Omega, existing outside time and space. I went from confusion to understanding how to more effectively interpret Scripture."*

For us men and for our salvation, He came down from Heaven. *"Jesus is not just a man who found His inner divinity to show us how to find ours. He came from Heaven and appeared to us — God in the flesh!"*

We believe in one Lord, Jesus Christ. *"This dispels the New Age lies of Christ consciousness, and ascended masters. Jesus wasn't an embodiment of an archetypal energy called Christ consciousness, an ascended master, or simply a master teacher/prophet. Jesus is the Son of God — His only Son — and has been with God since the beginning, outside of time and space. I went from abstracting and questioning to trusting, and now I completely choose to believe Jesus performed unexplainable miracles."*

Taking the Plunge

When you start to make changes in your life and orient yourself toward Christ, it manifests in a few different ways. Certain actions will indicate that you are actually making changes and trying to seek the Lord by doing things differently.

The major aspects of turning toward Christ are:

1. Actively seeking spiritual disciplines
2. Earnestly leaning into spiritual formation

Spiritual Disciplines

The main spiritual disciplines you should seek after include:

- Reading the Bible
- Participating in the sacraments
- Studying Scripture
- Memorizing Scripture
- Worshiping through music
- Fasting
- Prayer
- Solitude
- Fellowship
- Service
- Journaling

A Word of Caution on Disciplines

When you are freshly out of the occult and approach spiritual disciplines, there are a couple dangerous patterns I see that must be mentioned. Let's look at these now.

Put Down the Microphone

A popular spiritual discipline that should not be approached immediately after leaving the occult is evangelism. It can be very tempting for you to turn around and immediately start telling people about Jesus. Especially if you have a social media following, after your conversion you might be eager to grab a microphone and start teaching people about Christianity and/or the occult.

I caution against this for a few reasons:

- **The "falling away" risk factor**: If you are fresh to Christianity, it is imperative that you focus on the inward disciplines to become spiritually strengthened, demonstrate consistency, and go deeper in your faith before trying to step into a position of leadership.
- **Theologically ungrounded**: You are not yet theologically grounded, so to step into a position of teaching could mislead others, cause confusion, and actually increase your risk of falling away due to frustration. This also serves as a distraction that might prevent you from becoming grounded in sound theology, because you are focused on production and social engagement instead of interior spiritual disciplines and formational growth.
- **Spiritual warfare**: The enemy will do whatever he can at this point to draw you away from Christ. If you begin stepping into complex and often controversial conversations to evangelize others, it can open doors for discord and dissension, and this can lead you while you're already in a rocky state of mind and heart into depression or spiritual decay.
- **Worldview destabilization**: Your worldview is already in a state of destabilization. You actually need less pressure and distraction from your interior life and should be closing doors to things that could throw you into an even more destabilized worldview. Your goal should be worldview reformation at this point, not evangelism or apologetics.
- **The "look at me" factor**: The occult is all about the self. When you're coming out of the occult, you need to renounce that way

of thinking and work hard to reform through interior spiritual disciplines and formation. When you curb the desire to fuel your pride and stop putting yourself in the center, you can now turn your eyes to Christ. You need to listen and watch for Christ to move, not move yourself on the basis of your own human desires.

These are just a few reasons that you should put down the microphone when you're in the initial stages of leaving the occult. You need time to regroup and untangle your occult worldview before entering into certain ministries, especially those related to evangelism and media.

A point of hope is that God does have a lane for each person in the Body of Christ to build up the Kingdom of God. We are each called to our own lane. We must respect one another's lanes. We must also be intentional about listening to God's voice and make sure that the ministries we decide to engage in are ministries to which we are actually called.

Drop the Fascination with Spiritual Gifts

Another word of caution to anyone leaving the occult is to curb any curiosity toward using spiritual gifts. I actually tell people, "Rebuke the curiosity."

When you're coming out of the occult, you've likely just spent time playing with occult power in some capacity, sometimes over many years. If you aren't careful, your fascination with occult power can be redirected immediately toward alleged spiritual gifts. Some of the big ones that tend to pique an ex-occultist's curiosity are prophecy and healing. Getting wrapped up in studying these at this point in the journey is a big no-no! It's a distraction, and it's dangerous. You need to start with basic theological understanding and focus earnestly on foundational teachings, especially the gospel.

There are some significant differences between the Christian view of spiritual gifts and how they are interpreted or perceived by someone with an occult worldview. Here are just a few examples.

Christian worldview:

- **Prophecy**: declares the gospel of Christ and points people toward salvation and the coming of Our Lord Jesus Christ
- **Healing**: a miracle that occurs through intercessory prayer

Occult worldview:

- **Prophecy**: usurps occult powers to attempt to see the future; focuses on worldly events and that which is perishing and spiritually dead
- **Healing**: a miracle manifested by a human channeling occult power through their body and directed into another person or themselves

Often a person still locked in occult worldviews thinks that, since they've decided to become Christian, they should develop their new Christian "powers" because they have spiritual gifts. You can hear the occult nomenclature coming out of their mouths as they assert these desires. Obsession with spiritual gifts is a huge red flag for a new Christian coming out of the occult. I will often kindly redirect their inclinations away from such gifts toward study, the sacraments, and prayer.

Disclaimer: Spiritual gifts do not work at all like occult power. Spiritual gifts are given by the Holy Spirit for the building up of the Kingdom of God, and we as humans do not control the gifts in any way. God will make it clear to you what gifts you have and how He wants to use you for the building up of the Kingdom when the time is right, but you shouldn't seek out the gifts right after leaving the occult.

Very early on when I work with someone, I discuss the issue of worldview. If you can accept that you have a worldview that needs to be reformed, you'll accept that your thoughts and inspirations can lead you toward the occult because you haven't fully placed Jesus on the throne of your heart yet. Placing Jesus on the throne of your heart takes time and dedication to spiritual disciplines and formation.

I don't cover spiritual gifts at all in my foundational classes with ex-occultists because it's the last thing they need to be thinking about. The demonic is just waiting to draw you back into the occult through temptation and signs and wonders. Therefore, it is much more prudent for you to cut off any curiosity toward the paranormal and preternatural. You should be very cautious about approaching anything that might have a hint of occultic flavor to it. Remember, since demons pretend to be positive spiritual entities, any interest in that realm can lead you astray as you're getting freed of demonic influences. You will become more discerning as you mature in faith.

Initially, you must humble yourselves and earnestly drink the milk before trying to eat the steak.

> For every one who lives on milk is unskilled in the word of righteousness, for he is a child. But solid food is for the mature, for those who have their faculties trained by practice to distinguish good from evil. (Heb. 5:13–14)

As a new ex-occultist, you must realize that you have not yet gotten to a place where you can spiritually discern. You need to immerse yourself in Scripture for a while to reform your worldview and saturate your very being in the Faith. You should:

- Rebuke the curiosity
- Relinquish the desire for occult power
- Lock your eyes on Jesus
- Humble yourself and submit to the process
- Focus on interior spiritual disciplines

Spiritual Fortification

When you come out of the occult and surrender to Christ, you need to prepare pretty quickly to "enter the Woods." The phrase you should immediately remember is this: *Close the doors!* For a freshly surrendered-to-Christ ex-occultist, there are many open doors to the enemy. These should be assessed and then promptly closed. Here are three words to consider as you prepare to armor up and spiritually fortify yourself:

1. **Vigilance**: keeping careful watch for possible danger or difficulties (awareness)
2. **Focus**: adapting to the prevailing level of light and becoming able to see clearly (offensive strategy)
3. **Fortification**: a defensive wall to strengthen a place against attack (defensive strategy)

Within these aspects of armoring up, you should cut off ties to people and practices in the occult, and then take on spiritual formation and disciplines. On one hand, this cuts off temptation. On the other hand, this installs new, proper Christ-centered practices.

Spiritual Formation

There are three mission-critical words an ex-occultist needs to focus on at this early point in their journey:

- Promises
- Protection
- Inheritance

The enemy tries to obfuscate the truth about these three topics through the occult. The world and Satan will constantly throw lies at you to cover up the truth about your identity in Christ, and the occult utilizes identity theft avatars to confuse and distract you into denying God's promises, refusing God's protection, and ignoring God's inheritance.

If you believe these lies, you will find yourself journeying away from the path toward Christ.

As an ex-occultist, you must immerse yourself in understanding the biblical truths about these three concepts. Doing so will set you up early for success. It will help you get anchored to Christ and secure in you the desire for the spiritual disciplines and contemplative spiritual growth.

Scripture Memorization

A really great way to start to integrate the truths about the theological concepts surrounding God's promises, protection, and inheritance is to record yourself reading relevant Scripture passages out loud, and then play them back over time to memorize them. You can do this while driving in the car, or while going on a run. Let these Scripture passages become your anthems. There is no better way to wash out the enemy's voice and the stain of the occult than by washing your mind with Scripture as you lean into prayer, fasting, and the sacraments.

One thing that is especially important to consider when it comes to Scripture memorization for an ex-occultist: Scripture is not to be used as a "name it and claim it"–type deal. Quoting Scripture should not be approached as witchcraft. Speaking Scripture out loud does not manifest it or activate some kind of occult power. Scripture should not be used as an occult affirmation, as a means to speak something into existence, or as an attempt to access some good fortune through the inadequate means of merely saying words. All of these practices are evidence of an occult worldview.

The proper orientation of thought here is to accept that the Word of God is truth. Speaking Scripture out loud is saying something that is already true. From a spiritual warfare standpoint, it serves as a reminder of the truth; it can enhance our confidence in the truth and instill a sense of peace and hope as you focus on Christ.

Here are some key scriptural passages to study and consider memorizing:

Promises

- "Truly, truly, I say to you, he who hears my word and believes him who sent me, has eternal life; he does not come into judgment, but has passed from death to life." (John 5:24)
- "And my God will supply every need of yours according to his riches in glory in Christ Jesus." (Phil. 4:19)
- "Choose life, that you and your descendants may live, loving the LORD your God, obeying his voice, and cleaving to him; for he is your life and the length of your days, that you may dwell in the land which the LORD swore to your fathers, to Abraham, to Isaac, and to Jacob, to give them." (Deut. 30:20)
- "For all the promises of God find their Yes in him. That is why we utter the Amen through him, to the glory of God." (2 Cor. 1:20)
- "We know that in everything God works for good with those who love him, who are called according to his purpose." (Rom. 8:28)
- "But they who wait for the LORD shall renew their strength, they shall mount up with wings like eagles, they shall run and not be weary, they shall walk and not faint." (Isa. 40:31)
- "For the LORD God is a sun and shield; the LORD bestows favor and honor. No good thing does he withhold from those who walk uprightly." (Ps. 84:11)
- "Let us hold fast the confession of our hope without wavering, for he who promised is faithful." (Heb. 10:23)
- "For I know the plans I have for you, says the LORD, plans for welfare and not for evil, to give you a future and a hope." (Jer. 29:11)

- "This is the covenant that I will make with them after those days, says the Lord: I will put my laws on their hearts, and write them on their minds." (Heb. 10:16)
- "Peace I leave with you; my peace I give to you. Not as the world gives do I give to you. Let not your hearts be troubled, neither let them be afraid." (John 14:27)

Protection

- "I give them eternal life, and they shall never perish, and no one shall snatch them out of my hand." (John 10:28)
- "But the Lord is faithful; he will strengthen you and guard you from evil." (2 Thess. 3:3)
- "Be strong and of good courage, do not fear or be in dread of them, for it is the LORD your God who goes with you; he will not fail you or forsake you." (Deut. 31:6)
- "Fear not, for I am with you; be not dismayed, for I am your God; I will strengthen you, I will help you, I will uphold you with my victorious right hand." (Isa. 41:10)
- "Deliver me from my enemies, O my God, protect me from those who rise up against me." (Ps. 59:1)
- "But let all who take refuge in you rejoice, let them ever sing for joy! Spread your protection over them, that those who love your name may exult in you." (Ps. 5:11)
- "Many are the afflictions of the righteous; but the LORD delivers him out of them all." (Ps. 34:19)
- "God is our refuge and strength, a very present help in trouble." (Ps. 46:1)
- "Be merciful to me, O God, be merciful to me, for in you my soul takes refuge; in the shadow of your wings I will take refuge, till the storms of destruction pass by." (Ps. 57:1)

- "Though I walk in the midst of trouble, you preserve my life; you stretch out your hand against the wrath of my enemies, and your right hand delivers me." (Ps. 138:7)
- "My God, my rock, in whom I take refuge, my shield, and the horn of my salvation, my stronghold and my refuge, my savior; you save me from violence." (2 Sam. 22:3)
- "Even though I walk through the valley of the shadow of death, I fear no evil; for you are with me; your rod and your staff, they comfort me." (Ps. 23:4)
- "I lift up my eyes to the hills. From whence does my help come?" (Ps. 121:1)
- "The LORD will keep you from all evil; he will keep your life." (Ps. 121:7)

Inheritance

- "The Spirit himself bears witness with our spirit that we are children of God, and if children, then heirs, heirs of God and fellow heirs with Christ, provided we suffer with him in order that we may also be glorified with him." (Rom. 8:16–17)
- "Blessed be the God and Father of our Lord Jesus Christ! By his great mercy we have been born anew to a living hope through the resurrection of Jesus Christ from the dead, to an inheritance which is imperishable, undefiled, and unfading, kept in heaven for you, who by God's power are guarded through faith for a salvation ready to be revealed in the last time." (1 Pet. 1:3–5)

My Story

Immediately following my "gig is up" moment, I spent about two months in the In-Between. During that time, I generally wallowed in guilt and tried to figure out how to get myself out of the mess I was in, mentally, physically, emotionally, and spiritually. The In-Between for me was filled with nights of crying and praying to God to show me where I needed to turn. After two months of feeling lost and confused, I had a dream.

A Vision of Our Lady

I opened my eyes to find myself standing on a ship. All of my old friends from the occult stood around me, talking. I looked out across the ocean and beheld on the horizon a beautiful sunrise. A woman appeared in the sky, just to the right of the sun. My eyes filled with tears. It was Mary, glowing in vibrant colors of crimson, teal, and gold. She was emblazoned with color all around her, and she held her arms out to me in a loving embrace.

"Look! It's Mary!" I exclaimed to the others. They murmured in confusion and looked where I was pointing.

But they couldn't see her. I kept telling them to look, yet no matter what, they couldn't catch a glimpse of her. They lost interest and returned to their idle chatter.

"They can't see," I said, with pain and despair in my voice. I was so sad that they couldn't behold the most beautiful vision I had ever seen, right there in front of us. They didn't even seem to care. I clung to the image of Mary in the sky as long as the vision would allow. I felt hope welling up inside me, something I hadn't felt in a long time.

I woke up that morning repeating the words, "They can't see. They can't see." Mary's countenance was burned into my mind like strands of colorful light. I had a strength inside me that I had never experienced before. I could finally see through the occult fog, and I knew exactly what to do. I packed a single bag and prepared to head across the country. I was finally ready to leave it all behind.

I was going to a safe haven of strong Christians where I knew I could get the guidance and support I needed.

I got in the car and, protected by Mary's most blessed mantle, made my way out of the city.

17

ENTER: THE WOODS

Spiritual attacks increase. Persevere. Build new worldview.

The Woods are dark. The Woods are scary. Entering the Woods is the hardest and most treacherous part of the journey out of the occult.

In the Woods, there are many dangers. The greatest danger is the propensity to fall away. To give up. To stop leaning into faith. To return to one's prior state, which if returned to will be far worse than before.

How Do You Successfully Navigate the Woods?

In my experience working with people coming out of the occult, certain factors come into play regarding the success or failure of a person in the Woods.

Success Factors:

- **Humility**: You must renounce your pride over and over, turning to Christ so you can rewire your entire worldview.
- **Prayer**: Establishing a dedicated prayer life is paramount.
- **Christ-centered mindset**: If you try to lean on your own understanding in the Woods, things can go south very quickly. The enemy will use intrusive thoughts to throw you off the straight and narrow path. You must humble yourself and come back to the spiritual formation process again and again.
- **Perseverance**: You cannot get impatient and ask, "Is this over yet?" Most people start asking that immediately after entering the Woods, and I have to caution them to realize they are just getting started. Setting the proper expectations helps keep them from becoming fatigued.
- **Way of life**: You must develop a way of life, a spiritual formation plan, and continue to grow in faith.

What Do the Woods Look Like?

- Spiritual warfare and demonic attacks typically increase when you enter the Woods. This is because Satan loathes when an occultist comes to Christ, so he casts doubt and fear, trying to scare you into isolation, depression, and even suicide. He wants to intimidate you back into bondage. If that doesn't work, sometimes he might even try to kill you.
- You must stay the course, stay strong, become grounded in your faith, and persevere during this time of trauma and suffering.
- You might harbor intense guilt and sorrow during this time, as the magnitude of the truth washes over you and you realize just how much occult practices grieve the Lord.

- During this phase, you must focus on spiritual formation, worship, dedicated study, and the renewal of your mind.
- While you're in the process of shucking off an occult worldview, by the power of the Holy Spirit, you are also building a Christian worldview.
- Over time, as you learn to bring your thoughts and purposes captive to Christ, you begin to cast off the occult programming.

The One Thing Nobody Wants to Hear about Occult Deliverance

Occult deliverance is not fun.

Nobody wants to hear that something will require hard work and take dedication. We all want a quick and easy answer that will resolve whatever problem we face.

Quick, easy answers only temporarily resolve the symptom, but do nothing to get to the root cause, and they likewise do nothing to actually heal that root.

The same goes for deliverance.

Deliverance is not a parlor trick, nor is it something that happens easily or quickly for a person in occult bondage. It often takes years of dedication, and even still, the choice to lean into Jesus Christ actually has to be a complete worldview shift, a total lifestyle revolution, and a change of heart that extends into every aspect and moment of a person's life. It has to be a complete *metanoia* or spiritual change.

Often people in occult bondage don't want to hear this. Why? There are many reasons, but one reason relates to what I call the worldview tug-of-war.

Worldview Tug-of-War

When you have an occult worldview, you are programmed to seek occult solutions to problems. This includes attempts at shortcuts (divination/witchcraft), getting a result by harnessing occult power, and receiving information by accepting occult knowledge. These things seem to come really easily for you as a person working in concert with Satan (whether you realize that that is what you're doing is irrelevant).

Occult practices might seem easy, comforting, and benign when you're in bondage (because Satan has pulled the wool over your eyes). Suddenly, when you try to leave these practices behind, life becomes extremely hard.

Finding solutions to problems seems impossible. The enemy will attack and oppress you, making you feel like the world is crumbling around you. Because you've functioned for so long out of habitual witchcraft, you have cut off your communication with God. When you turn away from the occult, you are extremely disoriented. Instead of the telephone line to Satan, you are left wondering how to actually hear the voice of God and know what to do. Your old worldview has you seeking after lying synchronicities (satanic signs and wonders) that will only lead you further into bondage, so you are left completely confused about how to even walk with Christ. You might have trouble praying, and you will need to work over time and with dedication to understand how to pray, who God truly is, and how to hear His voice instead of Satan's.

Many anchors will still attempt to lead you back into the occult. The occult worldview is still in place and needs to be methodically dismantled over time — this cannot happen overnight or without experienced guidance.

Resist Impatience

When you begin to turn to Christ and away from occult practices, the enemy will do everything in his power to keep you from being able to see the truth of Christ.

He does this by drawing you back into the shiny veneer of the occult and appealing to your desires for occult power and knowledge.

At this stage you are not yet out of the Woods. You must persevere, remain vigilant, get anchored in the Word of God, further your spiritual formation, and stay the course!

Often, in the early stages of the Woods, you might start asking, "When is this going to be over? When will I be delivered already? Am I being punished by God?" This requires a mindset shift. Each step is part of the process, and you should celebrate each small victory. The Woods require you to slow way down and look at the small changes in your heart. You are about to go through a time of extreme closeness with the Lord, so you should cling to Him for dear life and enjoy this time of intense communion with God.

Even though the Woods are uncomfortable and scary, when you're in this stage, you are embarking on a new experience that you will actually hold dear for the rest of your life. The Lord will use everything you're going through for your sanctification, and you will likely be able to help others in the future. As you learn new things and experience new moments of God's grace and love, you should cherish each moment and revel in each chance to celebrate small wins. It's learning to take it day by day and step by step. I often encourage those I work with to ask God every morning, "Lord, what do you have for me today?" and then proceed with gratitude for the life they have hidden in Christ.

This is a great time to study the character of God so you can begin to understand who He is and start untangling your misconceptions about His nature and will.

Sin and Suffering

As you enter the Woods, you usually experience a tremendous amount of suffering. Whereas within an occult worldview, suffering is seen as "low-vibe" or an indicator of spiritual immaturity, the concept of suffering takes on a completely different meaning in a Christian worldview. This distinction must be emphasized to new Christians so that they can reorient their view of sin and suffering. I always begin with the concept of sin and moral culpability and then discuss the concept of suffering.

On Sin

Sometimes as a person enters the Woods, they will ask, "As Christians, when we lose the favor of God, is it because of sin in our lives? Is this how we lose His protection?" Here are a few Scripture passages and doctrinal principles that have proven successful in shifting this worldview toward a Christ-centered belief about sin.

> **Sin is a free choice made to step away from God.** "Sin is an offense against reason, truth, and right conscience; it is failure in genuine love for God and neighbor caused by a perverse attachment to certain goods. It wounds the nature of man and injures human solidarity. It has been defined as 'an utterance, a deed, or a desire contrary to the eternal law' " (*CCC*, 1849).
>
> **People can be handed over to their sin (again, this is because of our free will to choose whatever path we want).** "The one who is righteous by faith will live. The wrath of God is indeed being revealed from heaven against every impiety and wickedness of those who suppress the truth by their wickedness" (Rom. 1:17–18). "They became vain in their reasoning, and their senseless minds were darkened. While claiming to be wise, they became fools and exchanged the glory of the immortal God for the likeness of an image of mortal man or of birds or of four-legged animals or of snakes. Therefore, God handed them over to impurity through the lusts of their hearts for the mutual degradation of their bodies. They exchanged the truth of God for a lie" (Rom. 1:21–25).

Jesus suffered to take away our sin. "Therefore he had to be made like his brethren in every respect, so that he might become a merciful and faithful high priest in the service of God, to make expiation for the sins of the people. For because he himself has suffered and been tempted, he is able to help those who are tempted" (Heb. 2:17–18).

Sin is removed through the sacrament of Baptism. "The baptized have 'put on Christ.' Through the Holy Spirit, Baptism is a bath that purifies, justifies, and sanctifies.... By Baptism all sins are forgiven, original sin and all personal sins, as well as all punishment for sin. In those who have been reborn nothing remains that would impede their entry into the Kingdom of God, neither Adam's sin, nor personal sin, nor the consequences of sin, the gravest of which is separation from God" (*CCC*, 1227, 1263).

Sin is removed through the sacrament of Penance and Reconciliation. "Indeed the sacrament of Reconciliation with God brings about a true 'spiritual resurrection,' restoration of the dignity and blessings of the life of the children of God, of which the most precious is friendship with God. This sacrament reconciles us with the Church. Sin damages or even breaks fraternal communion. The sacrament of Penance repairs or restores it. In this sense it does not simply heal the one restored to ecclesial communion, but has also a revitalizing effect on the life of the Church which suffered from the sin of one of her members. Re-established or strengthened in the communion of saints, the sinner is made stronger by the exchange of spiritual goods among all the living members of the Body of Christ, whether still on pilgrimage or already in the heavenly homeland" (*CCC*, 1468–1469).

It is important for you to enter a state of grace and have a right relationship with God, coming back under His protection after straying so far away that you have been handed over to your sin. It's important for you to grasp that you *must* repent and lean into your faith to come under the Lord's mantle of protection. This is where appealing to the Blessed Virgin Mother to intercede on your behalf is highly efficacious. I always recommend a daily Rosary and developing a rich prayer life.

On Suffering

Some people ask, "Am I suffering because God has lost favor with me?" They might be questioning God's love and perfect care for them. They might be feeling abandoned and confused. Here are a few points of reflection that prove successful in shifting this worldview toward a Christ-centered belief on suffering.

Don't assume the worst. God has saved all of us through Jesus. He loves us so much that He gave us free will to choose Him or not. We never really lose "favor" with God. He loves us the same, now and forever. A negative perception about God's favor can indicate a need to look harder at oneself and reflect more deeply about God. God is God and worthy to be praised at all times with happy voices. This world is full of suffering, which is a result of the world currently being in a fallen state (see 1 Corinthians 13:12). At times, God does hand people over to their sin in hopes that they will repent. But we can't assume that suffering equals a lack of God's favor.

Jesus bore the weight. Jesus bore the spiritual weight of every single moment of every single sin that has ever been committed — past, present, and future. He experienced the spiritual weight of that sin in His very own body. He is not ignorant to our suffering, but actually carried more suffering in His own body than we could ever imagine, and He paid it all as the perfect propitiation for that sin. The debt has been canceled! Paid! Hallelujah!

Suffer well. Offer it up. Rejoice in suffering. If you are suffering because of your sin, you need to repent and be reconciled to God through Christ. If you are suffering for another reason, offer it up. We are sanctified by means of offering up our suffering. Suffering can be experienced as an act of worship, an act of unification with Christ. When you are suffering, pray. Unite with the Lord and intercede for others who suffer. Ask to bear the weight of suffering and offer it up for the downtrodden. Ask that the Lord use that suffering to reconcile sinners to Himself.

I've seen tremendous conversions occur when people embrace these perspectives on sin and suffering. There is a palpable shift in a person's entire spiritual countenance. Many of the people I work with come from environments where they've experienced extensive prolonged trauma and gut-wrenchingly tragic circumstances over the courses of their lives. When they come to Christ amid their pain and brokenness, they arrive at the concepts of moral culpability, sin, and suffering, and then incorporate those concepts into what they are learning about the Cross. They start to grasp just how critical Christ's sacrifice on the Cross was (and is), and they see the direct impact it has not only on their souls but on those around them.

Normally at this point, there's a dramatic shift toward forgiveness for transgressions and abuses committed against these people in the past. They stop harboring hatred and resentment toward those who harmed them and start to become aware of their own actions that took them away from communion with the Lord. They choose to offer their suffering to the Lord as a sanctifying practice and an act of worship. They begin to pray prayers of thanksgiving for the salvation of their souls.

Disclaimer: At this point, I sometimes see a surge in spiritual warfare. Demons might try to convince the person that they actually deserve to suffer and that God will never forgive them for what they have done. I direct them toward the sacraments and encourage them to really learn about the sanctifying power of receiving the Eucharist in faith and engaging in the sacrament of Reconciliation.

The Four-Step Liberation Strategy

I've developed a four-step process that is useful for freeing oneself from occult bondage. You will take these steps over and over until full liberation is achieved. Even with past deliverance from the occult, these steps are also experienced across the span of a lifetime for a child of God actively engaging in theosis. Often, as you engage in prayer, spiritual disciplines, and Scripture study, the Holy Spirit will convict you of something. You can move through these four steps to reform that sinful belief or practice, and the more you lean in, the more the Holy Spirit reveals. The Lord is gracious and loving. He doesn't throw everything at you at once. It takes time to get reformed and grounded in the Faith. Little by little, you are renewed. This is the process of sanctification.

Step 1: Reveal

Self-examination is the very first part of the liberation process.

- **Study.** Dredge up the past and current lies you know you need to release to Christ. Brainstorm the influences and circumstances.
- **Pinpoint.** Identify the lies from the enemy you have in your mind and make a list.
- **Organize.** Categorize these concepts into tiers to prioritize tackling the more significant first.
- **Tackle.** Go through an examination of conscience. You'll have a list of lies to renounce and sins to confess.

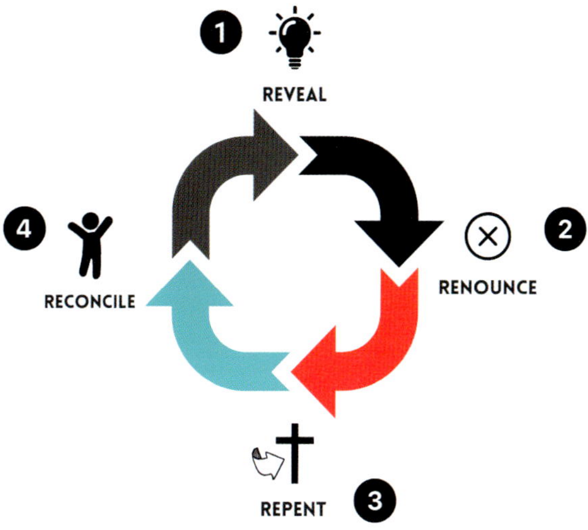

Dismantling occult anchors

I built an extensive framework to utilize in the liberation process called "Dismantling Anchors." We go through dismantling worldly and occult anchors. Dismantling occult anchors is the bread and butter of getting completely freed of the occult. It takes a lot of time and dedication, but it works. I could write an entire book on that framework, so I am just dropping the concept here so you understand the big picture of what is going on.

The process involves an in-depth look at a particular lie of the enemy, one that (in part) has locked you into occult bondage. When you accept a lie of the enemy and then engage in an occult sin, you've opened a doorway to the demonic and made a pact or agreement with the enemy. These pacts give Satan a warrant to enter your soul and oppress you. Seeking after and often receiving satanic signs and wonders draws you even further into the occult because now there is a belief attached to the lie. These lies can be extremely hard to dismantle because of the reinforcing signs of the demonic.

In this journey, you delve deep into how to place that lie in the occult anchoring process and then go through an in-depth exercise that helps you find out why that lie in particular has so deeply penetrated your soul. If you do not have the motivation to release the lie, you will not have the motivation to destroy the stronghold. The motivation has to be heartfelt and true. Desiring to rid oneself of suffering caused by demons is not the proper motive to finish this exercise with any success. It requires a soft heart and continual prayers for the indwelling of the Holy Spirit. This process goes nowhere without the guidance of the Holy Spirit.

This process is not a cakewalk. In fact, it is quite hard. Those who still hold occult worldviews and are filled with pride and idolatry are actually unable to approach this exercise. More prayer, spiritual formation, and yielding to spiritual disciplines are usually required.

Step 2: Renounce

To *renounce* means to abandon something, to declare one's abandonment of something. This is a very strong word! If you think about it, it means you have to be ready to run in the completely opposite direction from something you've previously held dear. You have to abandon any claim you have over it with such passion that you are ready to declare it publicly! This is not a half-hearted thing. No, this is a turning away with such fervor that there is confidence in your decision and motivation to let go firmly.

Breaking demonic pacts and agreements

Our worldview, feelings, attitudes, thoughts, behaviors, actions, and habits all tell a story. They tell us what we agree to in our day-to-day lives. Occultists use their minds, bodies, and spirits to say yes to demonic pacts and agreements. Demonic pacts are secured through sin. Even though you turn away from these practices and want to renounce them, the demons are still hanging around, waiting on the sidelines, ready to pounce at the next opportunity to influence you. They are hoping you can be influenced away from your newfound decision to turn toward Christ. If you have engaged in regular invocation and evocation through witchcraft, the demons remain because they've been invited in. They've been given a warrant to be there. They're in a relationship with you, and they don't want to let go of that relationship.

When you decide to leave the occult behind, the demons will try everything they can to stop you from making spiritual progress. Their top two goals at this stage are:

- to distract you from leaning into faith in Christ
- to draw you back into occult practices

Renunciation requires you to hold firm against the demonic. This is when the prayer and emotional support of seasoned Christians is most useful. When a person renounces demonic pacts, demons that have attachments to the person might retaliate through demonic vexation or obsession. This is why spiritual attacks ramp up when you are in the Woods. The demons have been given an eviction notice and are lashing out in an attempt to interfere in your life.

Perseverance is key. Here are a few case studies that demonstrate this phenomenon:

> **Demons of divination.** Debra made the decision to cut off her practice of tarot card reading. She woke up in the middle of the night, and an inspiration came into her mind telling her it was urgent for her to read tarot cards. A wave moved over her, bringing with it an influence of desire that felt palpably evil. Debra got up immediately and recognized this was a spiritual attack. She renounced tarot and divination out loud. She started reading Scripture aloud, and immediately the winds

around her house started to swirl. Others in the house were woken up by the Holy Spirit, came into Debra's room, and began reading Scripture with her until the attack subsided. Debra stood firmly against the demonic attack, affirming and strengthening the renunciation against the pact she had made.

Demons of synchronicity. When Bob attempted to cut off the practice of seeking number synchronicities, he went through a period of increased suffering. This manifested as sheer terror when he saw repeating numbers. Bob had the feeling of being plagued and teased by repeating number sequences on clocks, phones, license plates, and other things. He experienced panic attacks, paranoia, and fear of demonic intrusion, and he wondered if he was cursed. I taught Bob about the three different inspirations (human imagination, God, Satan) and gave him a firm grounding in each. I explained the concepts of pareidolia and apophenia. Pulling the afflicted from delusion and paranoia into reason through these concepts is often useful and calming. Because Bob was still harboring an occult worldview, he had a predisposition to seek hidden knowledge and signs and wonders. I gave him tools to function in his moments of panic. I instructed him to rebuke the curiosity. I told him, "It doesn't matter if the number sequence is a demonic sign or wonder, or a coincidence, or simply you seeking to find a pattern subconsciously. You need to rebuke and cut off the desire to know what it means — immediately, as soon as it happens. Say, 'I rebuke you, curiosity!' and turn your mind to Jesus." The turmoil caused by breaking off this practice finally subsided after weeks of rebuking the curiosity.

Demons of channeling. Fiona had engaged in channeled art creations. She built occult paintings during seances, sometimes using blood. As she started to go through the process of conforming her life to Christ, Fiona went into her basement and began pulling out the art so she could get rid of it. Immediately, she came under heavy demonic vexation in the form of dark bruises over her body, especially close to the occult tattoos she had. Because she was seeking to break attachments to these items and to the practice itself, the demons with whom she had made these pacts retaliated. Note that the purpose of a demon attaching to an item is to eventually attach to a person, so this must be considered when destroying occult objects. A person might be dealing with a double attachment situation — in part to the items, in part to the person. Even if items are disposed of, those demons might still be attached to the person. Solely getting rid of occult items is just one step in the process of severing ties to the demonic. The other side of this is repentance and continual turning toward the Lord to make sure the demonic pacts are totally severed. Once Fiona got rid of the items, cut off the practice of channeling, and continued in her faith walk, these demons stopped oppressing her. She is also in the process of having the tattoos removed.[25]

[25] She is now covered in the Blood of Jesus and, as mentioned, no longer experiences demonic oppression related to the tattoos. However, she has also chosen to remove the tattoos to demonstrate a Christian example that captures that she follows Jesus, and denies the glorification or promotion of the occult to any observer. There are many reasons why a person might choose to go ahead and move forward with removing occult tattoos after coming to Christ, but I find it prudent to mention it is not necessarily a requirement in bringing an end to any associated demonic oppression. I bring this up because I don't want anyone to fear that a tattoo might indicate a permanent demonic pact. Jesus breaks the chains whether or not a tattoo remains.

Step 3: Repent

Repent means "to turn from evil, and to turn to the good." The key concept here is *metanoia*, which is a change in your way of life resulting from penitence or spiritual conversion. This is a powerful concept that requires a complete shift in your heart, not just a half-ditch attempt to turn away from something. It's not enough to turn away from an occult practice; you must turn toward Jesus and invite the Holy Spirit in to be healed.

First, you have to assess what open doors you have to the occult in your life and start closing those doors for good. You should analyze your daily life and see which aspects you need to fortify — family, friends, work, leisure, and so forth. Remove people from your life who are stumbling blocks into the occult. You might also need to find other work if you're engaged in a career path that includes occult practices. After all this, you need to learn new habits and frequent new environments that will foster your relationship with Christ.

When it comes to renewal of your mind, it's important to have a procedure for handling intrusive thoughts and understanding how to actually lead them captive to the obedience of Christ. I invite people to use the Christ Captivity Exercise, which consists of four steps:

1. Take whatever intrusive thought, issue, or lie you are currently ruminating over and give it a name.
2. Find the antonym of that word, look it up in a concordance, and seek out passages in Scripture on the topic.
3. Pray and ask God for guidance, protection, and deliverance.
4. Build a clarity statement that describes the transformation and renewal of the mind that took place.

Here's an example of the Christ Captivity Exercise:

1. **Intrusive thought**: "I can't raise my kids to follow Christ if my husband isn't on board. I can't guide them on my own." Name: *impotence*.

2. **Antonym: strength**: "I can do all things in him who strengthens me" (Phil. 4:13); "He gives power to the faint, and to him who has no might he increases strength" (Isa. 40:29).
3. **Pray**: Ask for God's guidance, protection, and deliverance.
4. **Clarity statement**: "I went from feeling paralyzed and incapable of guiding my children to Christ without the participation of my husband to knowing that through prayer and faith, the Lord will strengthen me to minister to my children no matter who is or isn't involved."

Step 4: Reconcile

To *reconcile* means to re-establish a relationship with God. The Christian term *reconciliation* is the result of atonement. Reconciliation is the end of the estrangement caused by Original Sin between God and humanity.

Reconciliation conforms a person to Christ and opens up deeper levels of healing. You will become freer and freer as you lean into Christ and consistently pray for the indwelling of the Holy Spirit. You must intentionally renounce, repent, and reconcile as you build up the new worldview.

It is critical for you to have a local support system of mature Christians to help you through this process. Through prayer, the Holy Spirit reveals sin and distortions that need to be left at the foot of the Cross. As you examine your conscience and pray, these things come up. This is not the time to fall to condemnation or self-hatred. This is the time to renounce what needs to be renounced, repent from what needs to be destroyed by the Blood, and with sincerity of heart and firmness of mind, leave the darkness at Jesus' feet. The reconciliation a heart feels while going through the sanctification process and continually leaving sins behind to be conformed to God is a miracle. Lean into this process!

My Story

Enter: The Woods

I pulled into the farm and parked outside the house. Walking up to the door, I knew I was exactly where the Lord wanted me to be.

The door opened. My aunt stood in the doorway and embraced me. I was safe at last.

My aunt was a strong warrior for Christ with many years of experience helping people out of spiritual bondage.

And then my training began. She sat with me for hours and hours and hours, days upon days upon days — teaching me, showing me, explaining to me the nuances of Scripture and the Lord's love for me. She answered my questions and showed me how to search the Word. She was there to help me through the worst of the demonic battles and manifestations that beset me.

She taught me how to claim the protection of the shed Blood of Jesus. I started to declare that the pacts and agreements were void. I cried out to God through many nights of despair. The demonic nightmares were often so hard to bear that I would wake up sobbing in the middle of the night. I would wake up at five in the morning to pray, read, and memorize Scripture. I was becoming completely reoriented in this new world.

Yet I still had a lot of cloudiness and pride in me, tempting me to think I was ready to re-enter society and be done with everything from the past. But the truth was that I hadn't even begun yet. I thought that immersing myself in Scripture, spending time with the Lord, and learning what was true and false were enough.

I thought I was done with my healing, but I really didn't even know what healing was. I hadn't actually surrendered in a deeper way to Christ yet. I was doing all the things, but I wasn't letting Jesus show me what He had already done for me. I hadn't arrived at the heart of the reality that He was the one who had saved my life. I was still on the dark side of the veil, and in my pride and ignorance, I thought I was safe; I thought I was delivered. I also thought that if I fought back through writing, the demons wouldn't be able to stab at me anymore. I felt like I was ready to leave and go back into the world.

Oh, how wrong I was!

Not Ready, Not Healed

One fateful day, I thought I was safe to come out against the cult. I got up that morning after three nights of a particularly nasty witchcraft attack against me. I woke up with a plan to write a book to talk about my experiences. I desired to expose this satanic cult for what it was. Amid all the spellcasting and curses I was already struggling against, I decided I was ready to combat this coven with my newfound understanding of the armor of God. But I was not spiritually fortified. Because of my pride, I was not fully under the mantle of Christ. I was in the heart of the Woods.

As I got into my car that day, my family had a spiritual discernment that I should not be driving, but because they didn't want to come across as controlling, they second-guessed their feelings. At the exact time of the new moon, I passed through a cross street named Lunar Road and was hit by a car hurtling toward me at seventy miles an hour. The next thing I knew, I was lying on the side of the road in shock, shaking, shivering, and staring up at the sky. I was bleeding internally; my liver had been lacerated.

Darkest Part of the Woods

I never imagined that things could get worse. But little did I know I was steadfastly approaching the bottom of the well.

I was rushed to the hospital, and once there, as the doctors began working on me, I heard someone crying out hysterically. I was worried for them. I heard scissors and felt them against my skin as my clothing was being cut off. At some point I realized it was *my* voice crying out, and this was very concerning to me. Then I heard my aunt praying over me, and I felt her hand in mine. Tears streamed down my face. I felt completely broken. There was no fight left in me.

When I was released from the hospital and back at my aunt's farm, that night I wondered if I would ever be free of this curse. I lamented my idea to write the book that morning. I felt trapped and traumatized, too scared to go to sleep.

I finally fell asleep, but in the middle of the night, I woke up screaming in pain. My aunt burst into the room, threw her arms over me, and started praying loudly for deliverance. Across from her, looking directly at her, was a black demon with rage in its eyes. It gripped me across my body, its arms over me from the other side, mirroring my aunt's motion. It was freezing cold. It clutched me greedily as though it was claiming ownership. I watched in horror. Before I could say anything, my aunt's head snapped up from her intensely focused prayer, and she looked the demon right in the eyes.

"Satan, get your hands off of her!" my aunt shrieked, with a force that I will never forget. It was the Holy Spirit speaking through her with authority. The hair on my arms stood up with electricity.

I will never forget the moment those demonic arms that clutched my body immediately tensed at the words spoken with the authority of Christ. The room seemed to be suspended in silence. The arms then quickly loosened and slid off my body. The demon had let go and slunk back into the shadows. It was gone. The room immediately became calm. I started sobbing and embraced my aunt. She held me and rocked me to sleep.

I believe that was truly the darkest part of the Woods. The next night, the Lord would give me one word that, unbeknownst to me, would lead me directly into the arms of Jesus Christ.

The night after my aunt cast the demon out of my room, I fell asleep after more excruciating pain and prayers. This time, in the middle of the night, I shot up out of bed and shouted a word I'm not sure I had ever said before in my life.

"*DAMASCUS!*"

I stilled my body as the word seemed to hang in the air. It was dark, and I was confused. I looked around. It was quiet. *Damascus — what does that mean?* I thought. I sat there quietly for a few more minutes, but there were no demons in the room.

When I woke up the next day, I looked up the word *Damascus*. The Lord pointed my attention toward the Letter to the Romans. This was the path I needed to surrender in a deeper way to Christ — a way that would transform my reality and way of life completely.

18

EXIT: THE WOODS

Surrender to the love of Christ. Light at the end of the healing tunnel.

The sign that you are about to exit the Woods comes when you begin to surrender in a much deeper way to Christ. There is usually a turning point that opens your heart to deeper levels of healing and deliverance once you have been walking with the Lord over time and consistently engaging in the sacraments.

You will start to see the light at the end of the tunnel once you experience deeper levels of spiritual surrender to Jesus Christ. At this point, the attacks begin to decrease as you allow Jesus to fully break through into your life. This in turn takes you to much deeper levels of healing and deliverance.

Factors of Deep Surrender

There is a certain formula required for you to surrender to Christ in a way that carries you out of the Woods. I break it down by using the acronym C.H.R.I.S.T.

- Conviction of sin
- Humility
- Repentance
- Identification as belonging to Christ
- Submission to Christ's authority
- Trust in Christ

What are the factors that might hold you back from deep surrender?

- Denial of sin
- Pride
- Glorification of sin
- Conforming one's identity to lies instead of to Christ
- Rebellion, anarchy, disregard for authority
- Trust in the world

My Story

A Deep Level of Surrender

God was in the process of delivering me from the depths of the occult when I was overwhelmed by the truth of my salvation in Christ. I had no idea that when I heard about Jesus breaking chains, I would actually live to tell a real tale of release from the bondage of eternal slavery. Honestly, the experience is something I could probably spend the rest of my life trying to express properly and still I would never do it justice.

The pit of Hell had pretty much overtaken me when God chose to drag me out of it. There is literally no reason I am here today other than the fact that God had sovereign mercy upon my soul, called me out of the darkness, and, for His own good pleasure, delivered me from bondage. The moment of deep surrender to Christ I experienced while in the Woods broke the chains of the occult in my life.

> May the God of hope fill you with all joy and peace in believing, so that by the power of the Holy Spirit you may abound in hope. (Rom. 15:13)

Through the experience of growing in our faith, we begin to overflow with confidence in God's promises. There were three aspects of God's love that drove me into a deeper surrender to Christ's sovereignty, lordship, and authority over my life:

- **Surety**: When God was delivering me from the occult before I surrendered deeply to Christ
- **Remission**: When I started to see the invitation into a deeper relationship with Christ
- **Promise**: When I received God's grace and mercy and my salvation in Christ was fully revealed

Jesus Christ Is the Surety. I started to reflect on the fact that Jesus Christ is the surety of the New Covenant, and the Holy Spirit is the guarantee of the New Covenant.

> The Holy Spirit's transforming power in the liturgy hastens the coming of the kingdom and the consummation of the mystery of salvation. While we wait in hope he causes us really to anticipate the fullness of communion with the Holy Trinity. Sent by the Father who hears the epiclesis of the Church, the Spirit gives life to those who accept him and is, even now, the "guarantee" of their inheritance. (CCC, 1107)

The Holy Spirit makes active and present the mystery of Christ! This happens when we receive the Eucharist (see CCC, 1104–1107). When I was growing up, this was really hard to wrap my head around.

Why in the world would God come to earth as a man to rescue us from the powers of death and destruction and give us a way into the Kingdom? We don't deserve to be in His presence!

I didn't feel worthy of God's love, grace, or mercy at all. How could I accept something so perfect and wonderful? How could it even be true? Why should God, the most perfect, divine being of all, beyond space and time, give His grace . . . to me?

My "gig is up" moment brought me to the awareness of how disgusting my sin was, and I saw that I was living my life in utter rebellion against the God who created me. I looked at myself with not only disdain but incredulity and panic. I was offended by my actions. I hated myself.

Oh, the nights I spent sobbing, clutching the Bible, crying out to God and apologizing for all the ways I had failed Him. Because of my choices, I had walked away from God, over and over, to the point that I felt completely alone and unprotected. And that's when God called me and started baptizing me in His Word.

On my aunt's farm, as I learned about God's promises, I realized that God has a master plan. We are in the time of imperfection: we see through a glass darkly, a blurred reflection, an enigma. We aren't yet in the time of perfection when we will see reality face-to-face. We are quite literally living in a grace period, with God giving us free will to live up to His divine promises.

During this time, I underwent an intense spiritual transformation. I memorized Psalm 91, which became a kind of anthem for me. I recited it constantly as I spent hours and hours a day reading my Bible and listening for God's voice.

> Because he cleaves to me in love, I will deliver him;
> I will protect him, because he knows my name.
> When he calls to me, I will answer him;

> I will be with him in trouble,
> I will rescue him and honor him,
> With long life I will satisfy him,
> and show him my salvation. (Ps. 91:14–16)

Oh, what a lovely promise of God!

I began praying in earnest, "Jesus, if You are really here, if You really want to have a personal relationship with me, I pray that You will come into my life. I pray that You will reveal Yourself to me."

I felt foolish even praying this. As a former New Age author and speaker, I had spent years on stages promoting heretical ideas. I had no idea what was about to happen. When God pointed me toward the Letter to the Romans, things started to come to life. Everything started to change.

Jesus Christ Is the Remission. The Letter to the Romans explains with pointed clarity how Jesus had the power all along to break the evil strongholds that usurp control over our lives.

When God began baptizing me in the Word, He revealed two things to me:

- The reality and nature of demonic strongholds
- Idolatry

I started to see layers of truths around these two concepts.

I began to see how Jesus actually fit into this whole puzzle. You might want to stop and read all of Romans 5, but the following verses in particular are the ones that rewired every spiritual aspect of my being.

> Therefore as sin came into the world through one man and death through sin, and so death spread to all men because all men sinned— sin indeed was in the world before the law was given, but sin is not counted where there is no law. Yet death reigned from Adam to Moses, even over those whose sins were

> not like the transgression of Adam, who was a type of the one who was to come.
>
> But the free gift is not like the trespass. For if many died through one man's trespass, much more have the grace of God and the free gift in the grace of that one man Jesus Christ abounded for many. And the free gift is not like the effect of that one man's sin. For the judgment following one trespass brought condemnation, but the free gift following many trespasses brings justification. If, because of one man's trespass, death reigned through that one man, much more will those who receive the abundance of grace and the free *gift* of righteousness reign in life through the one man Jesus Christ. (Rom. 5:12–17, emphasis added)

One word jumped out at me with intense magnification: *gift*. Salvation, being restored in God's presence, leaving the world behind with all its lies, deceptions, and empty promises — could all of this really be a *gift*? Could it really be true?

My heart was softening after years of following worthless earthly philosophies only to find physical and spiritual death threatening to overtake me.

And God was clear: earthly philosophies are empty. Boy, I knew that to be true. He wants to destroy all the idols and worthless things. And aren't his thoughts much larger and greater than my thoughts? Why wouldn't the one who created me have a perfect plan I could trust? Why had I wasted so much time on the things of this earth, things that now were growing so dim in the presence of God, who was beckoning to me, calling me to Himself. Was this option, this gift, even offered to me? I considered myself to be the lowliest of all humans, a wretch of a person, really. I had spit on God's design and instead glorified myself and my own theories and reasonings.

My testimony was quite similar to Paul's, I discovered. A popular author spouting heretical nonsense, seeking to invalidate the truth of God. A warrior against God! I was prideful and oh-so-wrong.

I learned that God was calling me out of the darkness in much the same way He had called Paul on the road to Damascus. The world's philosophies now mocked me, throwing humiliation in my face for giving them such serious consideration for so long. The Jesus I had denied and persecuted now would be the one to save my soul and deliver me from slavery. God began to pulverize false beliefs from my consciousness and install the truth of Christ.

> We destroy arguments and every proud obstacle to the knowledge of God, and take every thought captive to obey Christ, being ready to punish every disobedience, when your obedience is complete. (2 Cor. 10:5–6)

Jesus Christ Is the Promise. As all the delusions faded through the wonderworking power of God, reality began to pour into my life. Here are some big truths I realized:

- The world will tell you there are all kinds of things you can do to deserve salvation. This is really the core lie that seeps into every other lie of the world.
- Throughout all my years of seeking truth, after going through all the various world religions and New Age beliefs, I came up short every time.
- Jesus Christ is the stumbling block when it comes to all other beliefs. He is quite literally the solution. He is the antithesis to all other falsities, because He is the Truth.
- It is God alone who restores. This should be a huge relief, but unfortunately, we have so much pride that we think we can do these things on our own, even things we aren't built to do.

I was standing on a hill when the truth broke into my life. My heart cracked open, and I felt the grace of God pour over me like warm water. I fell to my knees, and then I fell on my face. I literally felt the weight of my sin being lifted from my shoulders. It was so powerful that I could barely breathe. It was as though millions of pounds were being lifted from my back all at once. The weight of all the things I was never meant to carry vanished in an instant.

For the first time in my life, I knew that Jesus Christ was singing to me. The truth was singing to me from every single atom of every single living thing. I could hear it, feel it, breathe it! All bowed down to Him! I was a living part of His perfect design, and His plan was truly real. It was happening then, now, and throughout all time. It always was, is now, and ever will be. The truth is truth, completely separate from all the things we grapple with, all the imperfections in this human experience. All the things that don't make sense right now — they will all be revealed. There is an appointed time when all will be restored. Jesus broke the chains supernaturally, and we are in a time now between that event and the establishment of His Kingdom on this planet.

That's why we are told to hold fast without wavering to the hope we cherish, confess, and acknowledge. He who promised is reliable and faithful to His Word.

When the truth of Christ's salvation and the path forward into eternity hit me, I realized that the promises are *real*. I finally saw that everything was in its rightful place and there was nothing to worry about.

> Let us hold fast the confession of our hope without wavering, for he who promised is faithful; and let us consider how to stir up one another to love and good works, not neglecting to meet together, as is the habit of some, but encouraging one another, and all the more as you see the Day drawing near. (Heb. 10:23–25)

Breakthrough

After that moment of truth, I experienced a range of emotions I never knew existed. My heart began to move with the current of Christ's love. I saw so many situations where Christ was needed. I began to pray for Jesus to move in situations and places and people. I saw so many things around me that needed intercession, and I began praying constantly, at times weeping. Filled with His presence, I would feel such compassion for someone in need of His mercy. I was learning to submit to His will in my life because I could finally see how His will interacted with the present grace period on earth.

Soon after this, I had a breakthrough. It was time. Not my time, but God's time: He was calling me to return home.

19

After a period of deliverance, perseverance, and learning to walk with the Lord, He will remove your training wheels. You will exit the Woods and re-enter society, taking with you all you've learned. This re-entry takes time. There will be triggers that will remind you of occult trauma and deliverance trauma. You will have to learn how to function in society with your new identity in Christ. This can be clunky, awkward, and anxiety-inducing.

You are now ready to engage in social relationships in a larger way. With this will come new opportunities for growth and continued surrender to the sanctification process through the Holy Spirit. You'll get your sea legs as you become accustomed to the real world again after coming out of the nightmare.

There will be people who will negate your experiences, and this will bring more frustration — from potential negative reactions to persecution from non-Christians and Christians alike. Ex-occultists are often viewed as spiritual lepers and can be misunderstood by a society that actively engages in the blend and occult practices.

Dr. Thomas D. Williams, theologian, Rome bureau chief for *Breitbart News,* and author of *The Coming Christian Persecution,* describes the two primary aspects of persecution that ex-occultists might experience.

> An aggressive anti-Christian group, neo-atheists, [expresses] an aggressive hatred, more a rejection of God than a true disbelief [in Him]. There's a hatred there. There's something that's burning and very aggressive. I think that explains, in part, that kind of persecution, especially among those who convert to Christianity and embrace that. They are looked upon as traitors, as betrayers. They have gone over to something that many in this group feel to be very foul, very ugly, and very hateful.
>
> A second thing about this is really important: the whole question of spiritual warfare. A lot of people have experienced this in their own flesh, in their own lives. This is more than just a human thing. This is more than just person to person. This is about forces that are beyond us: occult forces, demonic forces. And this is something that, as Christians, we simply believe in. We know this to be true. And that spiritual warfare that goes on has real repercussions in the world we live in. And that hatred of God begins with Satan. It really does. It doesn't begin in the heart of the human being. It begins with the devil. And I think that this envy the devil feels toward God is especially burning when someone comes over

to Christ because the devil has lost someone he thought he held for his own.[26]

Often ex-occultists will be more equipped to discern occult red flags, bringing with the experience of that phenomenon sensitivity to Christians who soften or excuse occult worldviews, ideation, and practices. Ex-occultists will need to traverse such situations with love and care, yielding ever more to the Lord and listening to His call.

My Story

The Blend among Christians

After I re-entered society, many so-called Christians approached me to talk about my experiences. Many who claimed to be Catholic would assert that it was okay to use tarot cards as long as you were using them "for the right reasons." This confused me.

I had begun taking some courses at a seminary down the street from my house. I had a huge wakeup call when I realized that many students and professors were heavily engaged in utilizing the Enneagram. When I first heard them talking about it, it was new to me. But as I heard them discussing it during class one day, I quickly came to understand this was an occult tool — much like tarot cards. I did a bit of research and found that the Enneagram was indeed built and perpetuated by occultists who claimed to have channeled the methodology from spirits.

On a camping trip with some of the girls from the seminary, I listened as they were going on and on about the Enneagram. I finally opened my mouth and calmly explained that it was an occult methodology similar to other divination tools such as tarot or astrology. They all

[26] Teresa Yanaros and Thomas D. Williams, "Christian Persecution? What You NEED to Know," April 6, 2023, https://youtu.be/0jDu0OmNsBc.

immediately became very uncomfortable, and I was no longer invited to their camping retreats.

I became confused about the blend as I re-entered the world. I started to wonder if my convictions were too harsh. How could some Christians engage in occult practices and be okay, while I couldn't? I went to the store and bought a tarot deck. I put it on my bed and asked God, "What do you think about this, God? Is there a way to blend these practices with Christianity?"

After a few months of backsliding, getting slapped by the Holy Spirit through Scripture, I finally landed on the truth: There is no way to blend occult practices with Christianity. I also knew I needed to double down on removing from my life those who were still engaging in occult practices.

Healing through the Sacraments

I began to dismantle what I call my "big boss anchor." This is the foundational, stickiest lie a person integrates so deeply into their being that it's the hardest to dismantle. It's also the anchor point to which most of all the other occult anchors are tethered. My big boss anchor was tarot cards, and I finally started to break it down in a way that enabled me to see the truth clearly.

Engagement in the sacraments was a huge part of this for me. I would go to confession, my heart laid bare before Jesus, and cry for him to enter my heart and give me his strength. I would say, "Lord, I can't defeat these sins without your power. Please, God, give me clarity of mind and sincerity of heart to only desire your will in my life." At times I would walk out of confession being completely healed of a particular sin. It was like I had completely shifted and the sin didn't even occur to me anymore. Thank you, Jesus, for deliverance!

I also started to resuscitate and connect my identity in Christ through the Eucharist. One particular time, I received the Eucharist, went back to my pew, and knelt down. Suddenly, Christ's closeness hit me in a way I had never experienced before. My life passed before my eyes, and suddenly I was aware of the closeness I had experienced with Christ before being raped when I was fifteen.

I started to cry, so I left Mass and got in my car. Sobs from deep within me started to pour from my mouth. I felt completely held in the presence of God. I drove home and spent the next three hours on my couch, crying and feeling the presence of the Holy Spirit healing me from deep wounds. I realized that my relationship with Jesus had been damaged because of that rape. I felt a deep sense of loss and despair that so many years of walking with the Lord had been stolen from me because of this trauma. But at the same time, I felt the depths of Christ's love pouring over me as He covered and sanctified me in His Blood. He reminded me that I had never been alone. He had been with me all along.

All of these things together led to a much deeper realization of how to dismantle the final mental stronghold I had around the occult.

Big Boss Anchor Dismantled: Tarot Cards

After dismantling my big boss anchor, it would be a few years before I spoke in public about it. I wanted to make sure I was fully prepared to make that leap.

In June 2023, I filmed an educational video for a Catholic woman who was trying to get free of tarot cards.[27] After dismantling my big boss anchor, I was much more well-equipped to respond to her questions.

Marie had worked in occult stores for more than twenty years. She went through RCIA and became a Catholic in 2019. "It's been a journey," she told me. "Two steps forward, one step back. I've slipped

[27] Teresa Yanaros, "Are Tarot Cards Bad? Christian Perspective — 3 Facts to Know," June 4, 2023, https://youtu.be/tYGmMnu0iso.

many times but Jesus always brings me back. I'm slipping less these days, but I always pray that Jesus keeps me close."

Marie said realizing that deliverance is a process was one of the things that helped her most. She went on to say, "There's one aspect I'm addicted to, and that's divination. I know it's wrong, but I keep falling into it because it's a quick answer. I would appreciate your prayers."

When I asked her if there was any particular form of divination she was struggling against, she said, "Yes, tarot. I don't have any decks anymore, but I can easily access it on my phone." She was deeply involved in this practice. At one of the occult stores, she was the manager in charge of psychics, astrologers, and classes, and could get free readings whenever she wanted.

"Talk about idol worship," she said. "Going to cards instead of Christ — ugh."

I told Marie that it takes time to get free of occult ideation and to transform an occult worldview into a Christian worldview, so it was no surprise that she was struggling. Just cutting off a practice doesn't necessarily mean you've changed the way you feel or think, nor what you value. That's why you keep returning to it and can't seem to get free of it. There are still underlying issues you haven't reformed yet. The temptation is

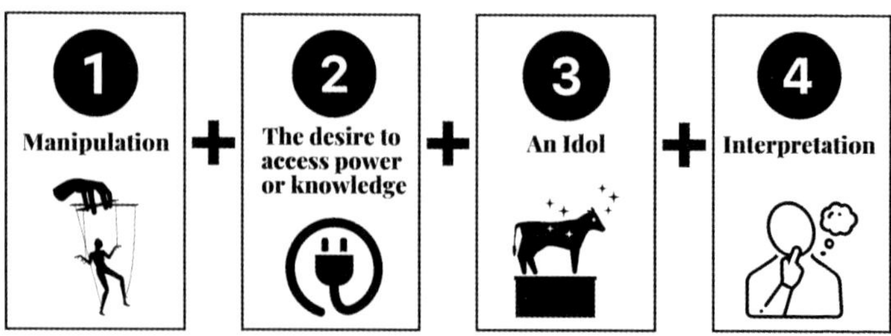

greater because you don't necessarily have the context yet for developing a heartfelt desire to cut that practice off and repent from it.

Defining Important Terms

Divination is "the seeking after knowledge of the future or hidden things by inadequate means. The means being inadequate, they must therefore be supplemented by some power which is represented all through history as coming from God's or evil spirits. Hence the word *divination* has a sinister signification."[28]

Divination can also be accompanied by seeking a sign or wonder and then interpreting it as the manifestation of whatever the particular desire was. When it comes to tarot cards, a person seeks to manipulate the cards to generate a desired result of receiving occult or hidden information through interpretation of the card's meanings. The person then perceives the interpretation as useful spiritual or life guidance. This is an attempt to control circumstances and outcomes by inadequate means; the key word here is *inadequate*. This gap is either filled through human imagination or through witchcraft.

Witchcraft is the attempt to control, manipulate, or generate a desired result by means of invocation (to call in) and/or evocation (to call forth) demonic forces (whether knowingly or unknowingly), combined with ritualistic practice. The act of reading tarot cards invites the demonic because the person is seeking occult knowledge by inadequate means.

I encouraged Marie to ask herself three questions that would help her cut off the practice of tarot once and for all.

[28] "Divination," *Catholic Encyclopedia*, https://www.newadvent.org/cathen/05048b.htm.

Question 1: Where does inspiration come from?

Inspiration comes from basically three places:

- The human mind (your imagination)
- God or the good angels
- Satan and the bad angels (demons)

The inspiration derived from reading tarot cards can come from two places: human understanding or demons. Because there's an interpretation factor when it comes to tarot cards, the inspiration is filtered through your own mind. This means you're leaning on human understanding and your own ability to derive meaning.

Does God speak through idols? The answer is no. Tarot is by definition an idol because it is a form of divination. So we know for a fact that God does not speak through tarot cards. God would not speak through anything that's going to lead people away from Him, nor would He draw them away from a relationship with Him.

Demons want to trick you into thinking you can use tarot cards to hear God speak. Satan wants you to believe tarot cards are useful and can help you in your spiritual journey. These are lies.

Question 2: Is this useful for my salvation?

Now that you've found where the inspiration comes from, you want to examine where that inspiration is leading. Is this inspiration useful for my soul's eternal salvation?

It is Jesus who delivers and saves us from sin, not some optimal life path we discover through tarot cards read through our own human interpretation. It's only the Word of God that awakens our hearts to the truth of Christ and turns our gazes away from the world. Consulting tarot cards idolizes the human mind as the means through which we can intuit the path to God. But when we talk about Christ as teacher, "His words are the utterance of the Divine person. He can internally illumine and move the minds of his hearers. He is the Eternal and infinite wisdom of God incarnate who cannot deceive and cannot be deceived."[29]

So, the question to ask yourself when considering the interpretation of tarot signs and symbols is this: "Does any interpretation of these signs and symbols actually lead me toward eternal life?" It goes back again to the issue of leaning on your human understanding instead of seeking what God has to say.

Is tarot useful for salvation? The answer is no. It keeps you fixated upon control and manipulation. It focuses you on trying to pull information out of a situation using your mind, and it leaves a gap there that cannot be filled. When you consult tarot cards, it causes you to become fixated upon the world, upon that which is seen. When you look at what God offers — eternal life — you're focused on what lies above, on that which is unseen. You're either in the world of the occult looking at tarot cards, which are temporal, or you're keeping your eyes locked on Christ, who is eternal.

Divination tools can only cause you to fixate upon that which is perishing and spiritually dead. That inspiration is not coming from God; it's coming from you or from demons.

Question 3: What am I seeking?

When you feel tempted to return to the tarot card deck, remind yourself that you're wanting some kind of quick fix; you're looking for an easy answer. Ask yourself, "What am I seeking? Comfort? Knowledge? Power? Healing? Am I seeking to control, to manipulate, to know?"

Then stop for a second and ask, "God, what do you have for me today? What do you want to show me regarding the circumstances in my life?"

[29] "Salvation," *Catholic Encyclopedia*, https://www.newadvent.org/cathen/13407a.htm.

Remember:

- God does not speak through tarot cards.
- God does not speak through idols.
- God does not use tarot cards to lead us to eternal life.

Now bring your attention back to what can lead you to eternal life. Where can you receive wisdom from above? You can turn to Scripture. Filling yourself with the Word of God is very beneficial. When you're trying to cut off one practice, you need to fill it with something else. Prayer is also really important.

Reading tarot cards is what I call *anti-prayer*. It literally cuts off prayer because, instead of seeking God, you're merely seeking your own understanding. You're choosing your own will instead of aligning it with God's will. You're actually choosing to worship an idol instead of worshiping God.

And the more you lean into tarot cards, the more darkened your understanding becomes.

- You become fixated on the things of this world.
- You elevate what your mind thinks.
- You develop an interest in what the demons are offering (if demons are involved).

That's why it's critical to understand the difference between seeking answers with tarot cards and seeking God.

How do you seek God?

- Pray.
- Immerse yourself in the Word.
- Receive the sacraments.
- Lean into spiritual formation and disciplines. Seek a solid spiritual director.
- Create new orthodox practices.

You might think, *I'm just going to stop this tarot practice.* But if you're not filling the void with something new — that is, a practice encouraged by Christ—that temptation to return to tarot can overrun you. It's important to introduce new practices.

I encouraged Marie to start journaling. This can take one's mind off one's desires and instead focus the person on what God is trying to say. This can totally transform one's perspective.

You begin to change your worldview by:

- Leaning into the process of completely letting go what you desire
- Filling yourself with Scripture
- Not allowing yourself to be stressed out and worried over what is to come
- Releasing yourself from the feeling that you need to know the future
- Abiding in Christ
- Trusting that what He has for you is for your ultimate good
- Surrendering to God's will in your life

Our desire to control and manipulate comes from a place of fear. We feel like we need to take something before it's taken from us. But God has an inheritance for you that cannot be shaken and cannot be moved.

I left Marie with this final thought: When you seek divination tools like tarot, you're back to thinking you can help yourself. Instead, engage in prayer and focus on your relationship with God. Know that He is here to help, guide, and protect you.

20

THE CALLING

Hear and heed the call from the Lord to build up the Kingdom.

Once you are spiritually formed, freed of occult bondage, and have a Christian worldview, the Lord will call you to use your God-given gifts to build up His Kingdom. There are many ways this can play out, but Christians living a Christ-centric life are called to love the Lord with all their heart, soul, and mind, and this compels them to serve the Lord and others. Sometimes, after the Lord reconciles the occult sins of the past, he might call you to minister to others in the Body of Christ who have been through something similar. This isn't always the case, but I have seen many people come out of the occult and feel called to help others who are getting freed of destructive belief systems.

After I was fully freed and anchored in a Christian worldview, I started fasting and praying about my calling. I knew in my heart that the

Lord had something for me, but I wasn't sure what. I felt the stirrings in my heart to help others, but I wanted to make sure I was yielding to the Lord's design for my life instead of forging ahead with my own will.

Soon after that, God called me into helping educate and free people from occult influences. It became apparent that there was a strong need for good education about the blend and occult deliverance. The spiritually afflicted needed to have an advocate to help spiritually form them as they were going through the deliverance process.

I started interviewing spiritually afflicted people from all over the world so that I could learn about their experiences. By the power of the Holy Spirit, this led me to form an academy where I could help draw Christians with a fervor for Christ out of bondage and into the fullness of their faith. I never imagined what a magnificently life-changing journey it would be.

I am beyond humbled to have witnessed so many individuals' transformations in Christ. I get to watch the Holy Spirit move through them in powerful ways, delivering them from bondage and awakening in them a deep passion and yearning for Jesus Christ. In the beginning of this book, you read Noelle's story; now I'll introduce you to Jamie.

The Yoga Controversy

In the previous chapter we discussed dismantling tarot in depth. I want to lay out another testimony that captures the dismantling of another popular practice, yoga. Before I introduce Jamie, I need to lay a bit of groundwork.

I appreciate that yoga might appear to some Christians as an unobjectionable practice, which is why I found it prudent to equip the reader first with all ten steps of the deliverance roadmap to effectively navigate the nuances around the topic, if it is indeed a point of offense or contention.

The question many people are asking is, "Can Christians practice yoga?" It's interesting to see how charged up and defensive some

Christians get when any evidence in the negative to this question is raised.

Throne of the Heart and Worldview

Now, as with most things we cover in this book, our discussion will center on one ultimate concept: worldview. The first thing to consider is what is at the very center of your worldview. I call this the Throne of the Heart.

THE THRONE OF THE HEART

What do you place on the throne of your heart? This will tell you what you value. If you are consistently placing Jesus on the throne of your heart, all of your life will pour out from the love of Christ that dwells within you. "Keep your heart with all vigilance, for from it flow the springs of life" (Prov. 4:23, ESV).

Harboring a Christian worldview will affect a great deal of things in your life. Considering the concept of worldview, let's analyze what pours out of the throne of your heart.

Should Christians Practice Yoga?

Now I am going to back up and give a brief spectrum of answers to the question "Can Christians practice yoga?" There are many different beliefs about the topic, ranging from:

"SPRINGS OF LIFE" FLOW CHART

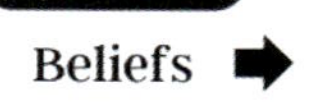
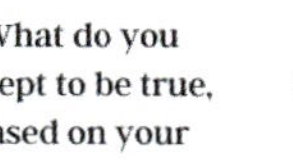
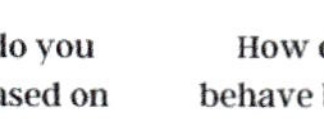

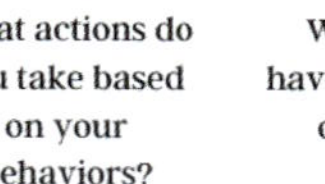

- **Absolutely not!** — Yoga is a form of worship that is Hindu in origin, and cannot be divorced from its spiritual origins. To try to separate the spiritual practice from the physical practice would be akin to going into a church and receiving the Eucharist because you are hungry for physical food and don't care about the spiritual aspect. This would be seen in Catholic circles as highly ignorant at least, and blasphemy at most.
- **Just do the physical, not the spiritual** — Some Christians believe you can stretch in a yoga class without engaging in the spiritual aspects of the practice.
- **Absolutely yes!** — Some Christians believe you can engage in yoga and receive both physical and spiritual benefits from the practice.

In terms of worldview, here are some considerations when it comes to yoga:

- The goal of yoga is achieving oneness with the divine through physical and mental practices, breathwork, and stretching. Do you believe that you can become spiritually advanced through yoga?
- Part of yoga is attempting to harness life force energy (*prana*). Are you called as a Christian to attempt to harness such powers? What does the Word warn us about the prince of the powers of the air?
- Can you engage in yoga and also place Jesus on the throne of your heart? Is this trying to serve two masters, Jesus and yourself as a god or healer? Can you do yoga without committing idolatry?
- Can you engage in yoga as a Christian and ignore the foundations of the spiritual nature of the practice while still adhering to God's Word? What does the Word say about sacrifice to idols? Is yoga a sacrifice to idols?

With research and reflection, each Christian should come up with their own answers to these questions. A common thing I hear is, "I am not at risk for getting into the occult. I can do yoga for stretching because I have no desire to get into the occult parts." While some classes that call themselves yoga classes aren't actually yoga, each person should understand what yoga is so they can understand fully what it is not.

It's also imperative to appreciate just how subversive Satan is when drawing people into his occult prison. This is why it's so important to seriously consider what one is doing through yoga. Do your due diligence to make sure you are steering clear of occult practices and don't just brush it off as something unimportant. Occult bondage always begins with pride. There are many slippery slopes that end up with a person in spiritual bondage, and I promise you, almost every single person who ends up in demonic chains started out by pridefully thinking it could never happen to them.

Full-blown occult bondage aside, all Christians should be wary of religious syncretism. People with spiritual blindness or pride toward these matters can often find themselves in situations where they are blending occult beliefs and practices in with Christianity because they are lukewarm and choosing ignorance about the nature of the belief or practice itself.

Worldview destabilization and slipping into the occult happens slowly, and you have learned the ins and outs of that framework in these pages. The practices and habits we engage in affect our thoughts, beliefs, and values, and vice versa. It is imperative to lead our thoughts and purposes captive to Christ. Leading our purposes to Christ means consistently setting our intention toward ensuring our practices glorify the Lord and aren't leading us astray from Him.

Jamie's Introduction

Yoga practitioners in the United States grew to 34 million people between 2010 and 2021, which is a 66 percent increase in just ten years.[30] It is estimated that yoga will be a $66.23 billion industry worldwide by 2027.

These statistics may not seem relevant to you, but given what I've been through, these trends keep me up at night and give me nightmares. I started as a Christian who believed yoga wasn't an issue for my Christian walk, only to trip fully down the rabbit hole of studying and practicing yoga deeply. I ended up possessed because of my involvement.

I get upset when my fellow Christians naively refuse to acknowledge the spiritual undergirding and dangers that lurk beneath the surface of yoga. Many pridefully assume that they can disconnect the spiritual practice from the physical; I too once believed this. Many Christians think that they can disassociate the spiritual origin of yoga from their own personal practice to justify physical benefits. This is a tragedy and leaves not only them, but those they have influence over, in danger. What we need to understand is that attempting to separate the physical from the spiritual components of yoga is actually truly impossible.

I have lived the consequences of choosing a lackadaisical approach to yoga. I thought I could live my life using my own judgment on how I engage in these other spiritual practices that were outside of the confines of Christianity. I was baptized. I went to church every Sunday. I was a very active member in my church. The Lord still did not spare me the punishment that I endured for engaging in these spiritual practices.

If you are a Christian reading this, I want to ask you to think about your Christian example. What example are we called to lead as Christians who love and follow the Lord Jesus? I feel, looking back, that not only was I an improper example of the Christian lifestyle, but I actually owe many people from my life as a yogi an apology: my previous yoga

30 "Participants in Yoga in the U.S. since 2008," https://www.statista.com/statistics/191625/participants-in-yoga-in-the-us-since-2008/.

instructor, and many people I came in contact with, both occultists and Christians alike. I endorsed and fueled the delusion and falsity that Christians could engage in yoga and also follow Jesus Christ.

Here is my story.

Gateway Factors

I wasn't raised Christian. I never saw my family turn to God during hardships, and as a result, I became hyper aware of what I could control. I saw the outcome of my life as resting on my shoulders alone. I perceived abandonment as a natural result in life. My mother and father divorced when I was very young due to my mother's own unhealed trauma and addiction. I continually battled depression and feelings of unworthiness.

From a young age, I had a deep desire to help others spiritually. Part of this was due to witnessing so much brokenness around me for so many years. I wanted to see healing for those I loved, and also for myself. I was passionate about the idea of helping others connect with a greater purpose. Clearly, I was a seeker. Little did I know, my seeking quickly and dangerously led me into the blend.

Occult Anchoring

I believed the lie that I could find God on my own, that an authority wasn't necessary to help guide me on the path to connecting to Jesus. I thought I had discovered the path, and that path was through yoga. Already having the propensity to believe I was in total control over my life, the occult ideation fit beautifully into my misguided belief system. I was uneducated theologically and saw no issue taking on these new practices with fervor and excitement.

I had always conflated well-being with physical fitness — the first wound of idolatry, as I now know it. After "simply" doing the physical practice of yoga, without understanding the spiritual undergirding that went along with it, something shifted. I specifically remember the day it happened. As I was driving home from the yoga center, I could feel this new, unknown presence. I perceived it as benevolent (spoiler alert: it wasn't benevolent). I was *sure* it was God. I began to conflate a demon associated with yoga with the Holy Spirit. (This anchor alone took me years to dismantle.) Soon after, I signed up for a yoga teacher training course. I earnestly and pridefully talked about my love for Jesus when introducing myself to all the students and teachers in that first training class.

Occult Snapping

At the time I was newly baptized in a nondenominational church. I had deep conversations with leading pastors to help me understand the faith better. I brought up my experience with yoga and the idea that it served to bring me closer to God. At the time, they were unable to provide any sort of explanation for my very real experience. They warned me that I should stay away from yoga, but unfortunately that wasn't enough of a deterrent to keep me away. What I had experienced was more powerful. Satanic signs and wonders typically are.

I rationalized that I was entering yoga teacher training to ascertain for myself what the truth was. One week in, I saw that the spiritual foundation of yoga didn't align with Holy Scripture. Still curious, I believed I was smart enough to decipher things on my own, so I continued. At the end of the training we were assigned a book report. I chose *Ask and It Is Given*, a book by Esther Hicks that she claimed was "channeled." I was hooked. I put my Bible away and didn't look at it for a decade.

Down the Rabbit Hole

I began to consume online content, books, and anything I could get my hands on that covered the Law of Attraction, synchronicity, reincarnation, Eastern philosophies, conspiracy media, and more. I was obsessively spending every minute of my free time researching. I was addicted.

I became so radicalized that I isolated myself from anyone whom I perceived not to be in "the know." I was infuriated that people in my life refused to see things the way I did. From my perception — based on the New Age conspiracy cult leaders I followed — there was a sinister plot to ensnare the sleeping masses who were unwilling to take a hard look at the facts of the reality of the world we live in. This "reality" stimulated un-Christian, fear-mongering, spiritually desolate, and ego-driven worldviews, but I didn't see it that way . . . at least not yet. In my estimation, those around me simply didn't want to do the spiritual work of New Age practices. I was so convinced of this that I broke off a two-year relationship, sold all my belongings, and moved to Hawaii to live with people who were aligned with these ideals. (I joined a cult.) The period from the start of the yoga teacher training to my move to Hawaii was in total just five months. I burned my entire life to the ground.

Shiny Veneer

Over the next decade, I moved back to the mainland, became a massage therapist, and married a Christian man. By this point, I was a full-fledged occultist. Even though I attended church with my family on Sundays, I believed the church wasn't necessary, that it had misunderstood the actual teachings of Christ and needed to be questioned. I would have told you that I believed Jesus was the Son of God, but I also would have told you that you could achieve His status by unlocking divinity from within. I believed in "Christ consciousness," along with a slew of other occult ideas about spirituality.

As a successful massage therapist by this point, I was invoking and evoking during sessions, practicing yoga, and deeply following lying synchronicities. I believed the lie that I could direct healing energy from God into another person through focused intention and ritual.

I enjoyed the thought of myself being a powerful co-creator with God, with access to spiritual power. I became drunk with the idea that I could direct power as I saw fit. Studiously, I took my job seriously. Satan had me right where he wanted me, and I was happy in my world of delusions. Or so I thought.

"Gig Is Up" Moment

After my son was born, I began attending church with greater curiosity about Scripture. I started teaching my son about the Bible, and my interest in what church had to offer increased. My heart softened. I started helping at the nursery, and after a mission trip, I decided to shut down my massage therapy practice. I was burned out and had a dream of starting a yoga studio. What was crazy, though, is that as soon as I slowed down, I started to actually pray to God. Truth be told, I thought I had been praying all along, but because of my occult worldview, it wasn't even close to prayer. What I had been doing was focusing my thoughts intently, keeping them locked in my mind, believing that I could will them into existence — what amounts to witchcraft. That barrier broke when I finally humbled myself and began asking God to tell me what He wanted for my life and, for the first time, not charging forward with what I thought I wanted.

I began praying with fervor. As I prayed for guidance, my health tanked. I experienced an unexplained chronic stomach illness that caused me to lose thirty-five pounds. I hit rock bottom. I believe now that the Lord was allowing my life to come to a screeching halt so I would stop doing things my way and hear His voice. At the time, though, I was enraged at God. I was under the impression I had this long-standing relationship with Him; I was doing all the things, so why was this happening?

One day I went outside and prayed, "God, I'm supposed to have your peace that surpasses understanding. I am doing everything in my power to be devout. I'm working so hard! You're going to have to tell me what's wrong." I had completely given up at that point. I was grappling deeply with the desire to understand where the Lord was calling me. I was in the throes of physical and emotional turmoil, but I hadn't yet identified this as spiritual oppression.

Less than a week later, I had an inspiration to check out a YouTube channel I hadn't checked in years. Teresa Yanaros had just released an interview with Monsignor Stephen Rossetti, an exorcist, to discuss occult bondage and deliverance. I watched as Teresa said to the exorcist, "I would like to talk a little bit about occult bondage. Can you first define occult practices and then explain a little bit about why these particular practices give Satan license to oppress people?"

As the priest began to answer, it was like the sound had completely gone away. Everything I thought I had known . . . it was a complete destabilization — the most gut-wrenching, guttural, convicting, collapsing moment I have ever experienced. *I was devastated.* My worldview had imploded. The earth-shattering realization hit me: *"I have given license to Satan to oppress me."* I was the source, the reason — it was my stupidity that had caused this intense suffering. The weight of reality, of my sin, destroyed me completely.

The In-Between

When I thought things couldn't get worse, God started throwing "gig is up" moments at me in quick succession, until things reached a fever pitch. The dam was about to break. I landed in the hospital. After I figured out that I was being spiritually attacked, the demons started to get emboldened. They began attacking me relentlessly. They must have known they were losing their grip on me. The memories of those moments still haunt me. I was inconsolable; I had never felt more lost.

The day I got home from the hospital, I watched Teresa's most recent video, which was actually her testimony of leaving the occult and coming to Christ. I realized that we were in the same diocese. She invited people to reach out to her, so I submitted the contact form. The next day, Teresa texted me, and we got on a phone call immediately.

At the end of our conversation, she asked me where I'd landed on yoga. I said I had been praying on it. She began to talk, but I tuned her out. She mentioned another video I should watch. She sent a link to the video, and we hung up. I begrudgingly opened it up. Two minutes into the video, I knew without a doubt that yoga was of the same substance and had to go. The next day, I called my business partner and told her I was no longer going to open the yoga studio. This was the first of many life-altering, heartbreaking, and painful decisions that I would come to make.

Colossians One Moment

Choosing Christ completely this time was my only option. I knew that if I ever wanted to survive this turmoil, it meant that absolutely nothing could stand in my way, no matter the cost. I hit new levels of contrition and awareness of my sin, and things began to pick up rapidly. I felt at this point like I was in a movie. First, I started Teresa's academy classes, and next, I began "closing the doors." There was no longer any gray area. Everything became black and white. I ended friendships and cut ties with people in close proximity to me who I knew were involved in the occult.

My partner and I became extremely serious about creating the time and space for me to study and do the long hours of hard work required to transform my occult worldview into a Christian worldview. With the Holy Spirit's guidance, Teresa's counsel, and the program she created lighting up a clear path forward, I clung to hope. We sold our house and moved. Through all of this, I hit deep waves of grief, as though I had totally lost my identity. God continued to prune and cut away at our lives. We became laser-focused on Him and on me gaining full freedom from this bondage. In the midst of all this, my husband lost his job unexpectedly, we left our church, and more relationships than I could count collapsed.

However, when it appeared on the outside that our lives were falling apart, we had never been more aligned in our values or clear that the Lord was present and leading us forward.

Enter: The Woods

Entering the Woods feels like you're walking into uncharted territory filled with a soup of emotions — the worst kind. There is despair, self-hatred, condemnation, self-recoil, self-distrust, unworthiness, hopelessness, confusion, and helplessness. It's like trying to learn how to walk or how to speak a new language. You feel like a newborn baby, completely dependent upon Scripture and the sacraments. In the Woods, I would oscillate between hopelessness and trusting in God's faithfulness. There were times when the depravity of my sin would overwhelm me and send me into fits of despair.

I clung to God. I was determined because when I experienced the truth of His faithfulness, it would pull me out of the dark recesses of Hell. I often woke up in the wee hours of the morning to read Scripture. It would speak of the demonic forces I was fighting, and God would do battle for me. It was like God was waging war on my behalf, and I was reading it in real time. Scripture became alive — God gave me eyes to see and ears to hear. Scripture hit me in my gut in new and profound ways I had never experienced before.

These are some of the things I experienced in the Woods:

- **Demonic obsession around numbers and synchronicity**: I was plagued by repeating numbers everywhere I looked. Whether it was my own inspirations, coincidence, or demonic attack, numbers seemed to tease and traumatize me to the point I thought I was losing my mind. The academy helped me to rebuke this and also detach from being triggered by these events.

- **Realizing a nasty demonic attachment**: I realized I had a particular demonic attachment that would engage me during times of intense rage and rumination. The demon would fuel whatever strong emotion I was feeling. I would ruminate on whatever the perceived wrong was, and then I would harbor that, harness it, invoke the demon, and deploy it, evoking that strong emotion toward whoever was involved. One night, the demon was actually revealed in my room, and I realized what was happening. It disturbed me deeply, and I began to cut this pact off through prayer and leaning into spiritual disciplines.
- **Learning how to forgive, including myself**: My thoughts would spiral with whatever strong emotion, but I learned to lead these thoughts to Christ, and I was able to look at things through the lens of His mercy and forgiveness. I learned to step out of my own perspective, approach situations with grace, and give others the benefit of the doubt.

Exit: The Woods

I knew I was exiting the Woods when:

- I began to take my thoughts captive with more discipline.
- I began to have more peace of mind.
- Lingering doubts of infiltration began to dissolve.
- Demonic attacks lessened.
- Nightmares became less frequent.
- My overall trust in God blossomed.
- My experience of faith and the sacraments was deepening.
- My confidence in my identity in Christ was increasing.

The World

Entering society after graduating from the academy and reforming my worldview was enlightening, to say the least — and not in a New Age way. Unfortunately, it became glaringly obvious to me that the blend was an issue present in the church I was attending. I was floored; I was appalled.

I was starting to appreciate the magnitude of the infiltration. I suddenly no longer felt like such a freak, like the odd man out. I wanted to warn the people I loved and those who might be open to my testimony about the spiritual depravity behind these practices.

The Calling

I shared my testimony on the *Spirit Sanctified* blog, which seeks to educate Christians on spiritual warfare — in particular, occult bondage and practices. I didn't want anybody else to make the same mistakes I'd made. I wanted to warn the people I loved, and I also felt responsible for those who had seen me endorsing the occult for so many years. I wanted to publicly take responsibility for my wrongs. I'm glad I did this.

In my eyes, sharing my testimony was a massive success. It got many views. People read it. It was on the radar. At the end of the day, I couldn't ask for anything more than for the Body of Christ to understand that this is a problem. And whether it spoke to them, someone they knew, or someone in the future whom they may know, my testimony served as a point of reference, a seed that could help them navigate how to speak into these situations going forward.

I am now dedicated to speaking to this demographic. I realize now that I have a calling to work in this ministry and help advocate for those in bondage. Praise God, I was fully delivered from my occult bondage — it was a massive relief!

Jamie's Advice

Trust in the Divine Mercy. "Jesus, I trust in You." Let this profound and simple prayer pour over you and be your battle cry. This is a marathon and not a sprint. You have to endure to the end. This requires mental fortitude, so psych yourself up and do not settle for anything less than crossing the finish line. It's okay to be uncomfortable. Flush out the noise and focus on the task at hand.

Memorize Scripture. The Word is your weapon. It's your sword. It's your shield. It holds and contains the power of God to defeat the enemy. Scripture is your battle cry. The Lord will use Scripture to speak to you in your darkest moments. Scripture can speak directly to what you are experiencing in the most intimate way, reminding you and showing you that God is with you. Memorizing Scripture allows you to be able to combat the enemy in the moment, effectively and swiftly.

Pray the Rosary. Mary is the mother of God! She has a very special place in the Kingdom of Heaven. Lean into learning how to honor and love her. She advocates for *all* her children. Study sound theology around praying the Rosary and Mary's powerful intercession. This is a game changer.

Be assured. When you are experiencing a breakdown, trust that on the other side, there is a breakthrough! Actively look for it. I witnessed this multiple times in my own struggles of leaving the occult, as well as after deliverance. There is always a silver lining. St. Paul tells us, "We know that in everything God works for good with those who love him, who are called according to his purpose" (Rom. 8:28).

21

Battle Cry

"Jesus, I Trust in You!"

One night, during the very first week after launching the academy, I was about to fall asleep. The image of a woman flashed through my mind and I heard the name "Lady Faustina." I was so tired I debated just going to sleep, but I knew if I didn't write this name down, I would forget it, so I pulled out my phone and entered it in my notes app. I pulled up the browser and searched for "Lady Faustina." I was shocked — there was an image of the exact woman I had just seen in my mind. I made a mental note to research her the next day.

In the middle of the night, the Holy Spirit woke me up with a design for a rosary. I got up, wide awake, and built a rosary. I had all the prayers in my head, and I wrote them down. It was all centered around prayers for deliverance for the women in the academy. At one point I had a fleeting concern that this might be sacrilegious; I wasn't sure if Rosaries had to always be in the proper Marian form, or if it was wrong to create something different.

The next day, I started to learn about St. Faustina. I also learned that there were things called *chaplets,* and that sometimes saints were given them to help people pray and intercede for a certain thing. This alleviated my concerns from the night before. I named my chaplet the "Deliverance Chaplet." I shared it with the academy students, and they began praying this along with their daily Rosaries.

I didn't share the experience with St. Faustina because I didn't feel it was prudent to share at that time. I did tell some priests about it to make sure I wasn't being deceived by some spirit pretending to be a saint. Because this was a solitary incident and there was no further engagement, it seemed to be safe enough. I made sure not to elevate the experience or idolize it. I just made a note of it and moved on.

Months later, St. Faustina started popping up everywhere. One student had a vision of the Divine Mercy; she looked up the image of Jesus and discovered it was a thing. And then she started learning about St. Faustina. Multiple women, directly preceding deliverance, all without having knowledge of any other students' experiences, were drawn to the Divine Mercy. This helped them to trust in Jesus and fully surrender to Him.

It all suddenly converged in a giant conversation about this beloved saint we had been studying and following. This opened up a conversation about how surrender and trust were instrumental in deliverance.

"Jesus, I trust in You!" became our battle cry.

I was invited to attend a training in Vatican City. On my last day there, I was eating lunch with some friends, and one of them mentioned they were going to walk down the street to the Divine Mercy Chapel. Beyond excited, I went with them, telling them stories about how instrumental St. Faustina's teachings about Divine Mercy had been in changing the lives of many women around the world. As we approached the church, a newly married couple stepped out, and the crowd threw rice into the sky. We all had tears in our eyes as we walked around the side of the building and went in the side door.

Suddenly, I was face-to-face with the image of Our Lord, the Divine Mercy. Grace and mercy poured out from Him to all the world. As I knelt in front of Jesus, I reflected on all that was behind me, and all that lay before me on my journey to finally, one day, behold the precious face of my Lord and Savior, Jesus Christ.

The Importance of Advocacy

Advocating for the spiritually afflicted is a necessity in these times. I want to end by sharing Noelle's and Jamie's perspectives on advocacy to showcase how mentoring someone going through deliverance can light the way to spiritually multiply the Kingdom of God and inspire new advocates to stand up and help others out of the darkness and into the light.

Noelle's Perspective on Advocacy

In my case, I would have been completely lost without having Teresa as my mentor and friend. To leave the New Age and become a newborn Christian requires a unique mentorship. Not every priest is trained in this field, nor do they have time to provide such intimate mentoring that requires special tools and teachings. (I'm sure there are priests who can offer this; however, in my country it seems quite rare, even impossible.)

A unique mentorship

Teresa was there for me before the program even started. We had Zoom calls and frequent e-mail contact. She gave me a list of prayers I could incorporate into my daily life that would prepare me for spiritual warfare. She often checked in with me to see how I was doing in general, because I was very isolated and she knew I was under more attack. She also asked her strong Christian friends to pray for me. I was flooded with gratitude when she told me that. To think there was somebody on the other side of the world caring so much about me and my deliverance! To experience the Body of Christ so early in my journey truly did something to my heart and the dedication I had to become a Christian.

The academy program itself involved two weekly calls, during which we would not only learn about whatever was on the study table that day but also ask questions and share our homework. Sometimes the days in between calls were so intense and I would fall back into doubt because of heavy intrusive thoughts and the weight of being oppressed.

These weekly calls gave me hope and strength to continue, because I knew:

- Others were in the same situation, and we could motivate each other.
- Teresa had gone through it and made it to the other side.

Aside from the calls, the academy members could share the clarity we gained and ask questions about what we were studying or things that seemed important that came up for us outside of the program. Depending on the topic, we were also able to have solo calls and could message back and forth, even daily. Sometimes Teresa would be able to spot a stronghold or occult ideation that needed to be reformed, and she would encourage us to either stop something, close a door because of a distraction, dive deeper into certain exercises to get theologically grounded again, or dismantle and research on a specific occult anchor. Sometimes we would spend hours digging deeper into what the root of the stronghold was.

The renewal of the mind can be very tricky and challenging for someone coming out of the New Age. To do it alone is dangerous, because the tendency to lean on one's own understanding is high, and demonic strongholds can be hard to see; some are harder to spot than others. If you have nobody to tell you what you need to dismantle, give you specific passages to read in the Bible, tell you what to do a word study on, or suggest specific prayers to you, the odds of backsliding are very high.

Because of the intensity of the process of deliverance itself, the suffering and the wish for it to be over can be magnified. One of the reasons I was able to persevere was that I had a mentor who showed me where I was in the journey and reminded me that I could continue to grow. Teresa provided constant encouragement to keep moving forward — that there was an end to the Woods. But she also taught me that, whatever stage I was in, it was important to surrender to God's timing and trust that He had a greater plan. I became grounded in the idea that sanctification is a lifelong process, and I learned to focus on being tethered to Christ every moment of every day.

Another aspect I want to touch on is the "rehab factor." Being post-deliverance can feel as isolating as being in the midst of oppression. To figure out this world and your place in it can be an overwhelming task. If you have an advocate who can validate the states you are in, it can be strengthening, encouraging, and useful in discerning what is important and what is not at that stage.

Jamie's Perspective on Advocacy

The importance of having someone come alongside and mentor to the afflicted cannot be overemphasized. I don't know where I'd be today if Teresa hadn't answered the call to help others in bondage in the many ways she has.

During this time, it wasn't someone speaking over my head that served me. It was Teresa meeting me where I was at. She was not only a spiritual mentor to me who coached me out of my incorrect theological foundation; she also spent time with me as a friend. She got to know me and my family. Unlike others in my life at the time, she was willing to walk alongside me in every way humanly possible. She wasn't afraid of the demons — her actions demonstrated clearly that she believed and trusted that God was bigger. The number of hours she poured into loving and coaching me is a debt I can never repay. It reminds me of Jesus and the type of love He had when He walked with and mentored His own disciples.

While I was going through the academy, early on Teresa began coming to me for advice about organization and operational and structural concepts. I didn't realize it until later, but I was helping her by sharing my observations. I began paying closer attention and taking notes, observing not only Teresa and myself, but also the other women in the academy as well. We all had similar questions, concerns, doubts, and thought patterns. It naturally became the perfect opportunity for me to learn all I could about this process. It struck me how similar all of our stories were, and I was floored to learn there is a common denominator at play. The combination of these events stirred a deep interest in me.

There was a natural progression from being a student to taking on a management role. During this time, it was a great consolation for me to dive deeper into understanding the nuances of occult bondage and deliverance. I spent many hours in conversation with Teresa dissecting everything about these topics. I felt like God was redeeming my passionate personality and rooting it in a love for Jesus Christ and others.

By being in the Woods, I had gained an intimate understanding of what it took to persevere through them. I had developed a steadily growing love for the sacraments and continued to develop a rock-solid formation in Christ. This opened up a strong desire in me to come out on the other end and advocate for others. Even before I was fully free, God gave me opportunities to live out this calling. I have been able to work with Teresa and learn firsthand exactly what advocacy looks like. The value I have gained from this experience is irreplaceable. The entire saga has been and will always be one of the biggest blessings in my life.

In my mind, advocacy for the afflicted isn't rocket science, but it does require effort. It can be as simple as taking time and offering prayers or penance on behalf of the afflicted, or you can take a more active role by educating yourself on the topics covered within this book. A big factor in effective advocacy is living in the fullness of the Faith. The afflicted need true healing, the type of healing that comes from God alone. This healing journey includes sacramental worship, a proper theological foundation, and a strong Christian support system. Becoming educated on the fullness of the Faith is crucial.

Teresa condensed all of her experience and research, synthesizing these dense topics into a deliverance roadmap. If you are called to become an advocate for the spiritually afflicted, immerse yourself in the concepts presented here. Coupled with a strong faith, this is the beginning of being a hands-on advocate. I'm blessed to be here, being a part of this community for those who need a light in the darkness — who need to be told, "No, you are not a spiritual leper. You are a sinner, just like me."

Author's Note: Lock Your Eyes on Jesus Christ

Thank you for taking the time to dive into and grasp the unique nuances of occult anchoring and deliverance. The most important thing to remember is that God is sovereign over all things and the Blood of Jesus Christ breaks the chains. Lock your eyes on Jesus Christ. Cling to Him. He is the Way, the Truth, and the Life.

If you are struggling to break free from the occult, please do not attempt to go it alone. Seek out local spiritual direction and help as soon as you can. The enemy wants to keep you isolated from others. Jesus calls us into communion with Him. He also calls us into community with one another.

If you need immediate assistance, contact your diocesan office and ask to get in touch with someone who can help you. If you come up short, contact SpiritSancified.com. You are not alone.

About the Author

Teresa Yanaros, a degreed journalist and devout Catholic, is dedicated to addressing the growing trend of disaffiliation with religion, where many turn to "spiritual but not religious" ideologies, leading to New Age and occult practices. Earlier in her career, Yanaros was a successful author and speaker, exploring modern American spiritualism and attempting to reconcile it with Christianity before experiencing a radical deliverance from occult deception. Now, she coaches ex–New Agers returning to Christ and provides Catholics with the tools to resist cultural traps. Through her growing ministry of online resources, classes, and YouTube videos and her blog, *Spirit Sanctified*, Yanaros helps Christians stand firm against deception.

Sophia Institute

Sophia Institute is a nonprofit institution that seeks to nurture the spiritual, moral, and cultural life of souls and to spread the gospel of Christ in conformity with the authentic teachings of the Roman Catholic Church.

Sophia Institute Press fulfills this mission by offering translations, reprints, and new publications that afford readers a rich source of the enduring wisdom of mankind.

Sophia Institute also operates the popular online resource CatholicExchange.com. *Catholic Exchange* provides world news from a Catholic perspective as well as daily devotionals and articles that will help readers to grow in holiness and live a life consistent with the teachings of the Church.

In 2013, Sophia Institute launched Sophia Teachers to renew and rebuild Catholic culture through service to Catholic education. With the goal of nurturing the spiritual, moral, and cultural life of souls, and an abiding respect for the role and work of teachers, we strive to provide materials and programs that are at once enlightening to the mind and ennobling to the heart; faithful and complete, as well as useful and practical.

Sophia Institute gratefully recognizes the Solidarity Association for preserving and encouraging the growth of our apostolate over the course of many years. Without their generous and timely support, this book would not be in your hands.

www.SophiaInstitute.com
www.CatholicExchange.com
www.SophiaTeachers.org

Sophia Institute Press is a registered trademark of Sophia Institute.
Sophia Institute is a tax-exempt institution as defined by the
Internal Revenue Code, Section 501(c)(3). Tax ID 22-2548708.